GUIDE TO ESTABLISHING AND OPERATING DAY CARE CENTERS FOR YOUNG CHILDREN

by Dorothy B. Boguslawski

revised and updated by Brenda Coakley
and Marjorie Kopp

Child Welfare League of America
Washington, DC

CHILD WELFARE LEAGUE OF AMERICA, INC.
440 First Street, NW, Suite 310, Washington, DC 20001-2085

CURRENT PRINTING (last digit)
10 9 8 7 6 5 4 3 2 1

Cover and text design by Jennifer Riggs

Printed in the United States of America

ISBN # 0–87868–032-2

Contents

Health, Hygiene, and Safety Issues

Relationships between Parents and Day Care Center Staff

Appendix A: Suggested Furnishings, Equipment, and Supplies

Appendix C: Organizations Publishing Resource Materials
on Child Day Care Centers and Programs

Introduction

Throughout the world today many young children are living under conditions that fail to ensure their healthy growth and development. Despite the vast body of knowledge about child development available to us, our contemporary culture has created situations that often make it difficult—and sometimes even impossible—for a family to meet all of a child's growth needs. The problems of child care cut across all income levels, all segments of the community, and all regions of the country. They are found in families of every race and ethnic origin, in urban families and in rural families.

Urban living, with its small apartments, elevators, dangerous streets, and lack of easily accessible outdoor play space, restricts young children in their bodily movements, in their natural desire to explore the world, and in their wish to seek out other children for companionship. In most large cities, there is a shortage of good housing at modest rentals; as a consequence, many children live in homes that do not afford adequate environments for healthy development. The need for parents to work away from home frequently leaves children unsupervised and unprotected, or requires that they be cared for during most of their waking hours by someone other than their parents. Because of the mobility of American families, there are often no relatives or even friends to share in the task of child care. Poverty, a reality of everyday living for 23% of America's children under six (or five million children living in families with incomes below the poverty line) often deprives children of adequate nutrition and medical attention. Marital tensions, divorce, desertion, and absence of marriage make family life less than ideal for many children.

The preschool child is especially vulnerable. Between birth and age six the foundations of health and character are established. During these years the child grows and changes rapidly, and how the young child develops will be determined to a great extent by the environment.

There is no second chance at childhood. It comes and goes quickly. Growing children cannot wait until they are older for the things they need now. Later will be too late. If they do not get sufficient food and protection from disease when they are young, they may not even live to receive everything we would want them to have later. If they do not have the chance early in life for the normal development of their minds, their bodies, and their relationships to others, no one can ever make it up to them. The years of their lives when they are most impressionable, when they are most eager and ready to learn, will have been lost beyond recall.

Most parents today are aware of the importance of these early years in their children's lives. More and more, they look to the community to supply a variety of child care services to supplement their own efforts in helping their children grow into healthy, happy, responsible adults. It is widely accepted that children grow best in the environment of their own families. It is just beginning to be widely accepted that in our present society parents must be able to call on outside resources to help them in the job of being parents. This does not mean that family life has broken down; it does mean that our social structure has changed, that new social inventions are required to fit the family's needs in this new society.

Most communities think of themselves as being more or less prepared to protect children from neglect and abuse and to provide substitute care when full-time care outside the home is necessary for a child's well-being. But most parents do not want to give up their children and have no intention of doing so. What they want and need and ask for are services to help them do a job that is becoming more and more difficult in our complicated society—being competent parents. There has been a lag on the part of many communities in recognizing this fact and in providing such help.

Today, families require a variety of supplementary child care services, dependable both in continuity and in quality. If the growth needs of children are to be met, these services must be offered to families on all income levels, regardless of their ability to pay.

The supplementary service parents most frequently turn to, when it is available, is some form of day care. Day care is not new. Traditionally, such supplementary, part-time care was usually provided by relatives—

grandmothers, aunts, or older brothers or sisters; often it was provided by neighbors (with or without compensation), and sometimes by housekeepers, au pairs, or nannies. In this country, group day care has been offered for well over a hundred years, on a limited basis, by community-based nonprofit organizations, by individuals, and more recently by schools, government agencies, employers, and for-profit corporations. Group day care programs have many different names—day care centers, child care centers, preschools, nursery schools, kindergartens, play groups, and, under Operation Head Start, child development centers.

The purposes of these day care services are as varied as their auspices. Some have a purely custodial purpose—to keep children off the streets and out of danger; many were established to enable parents to work. Some have the specific goal of facilitating child development and education for the preschool child, and others have been established as one of the community's child welfare services. Some day care providers, regardless of auspices or stated purpose, are aware of children's needs and the importance of their relationships to their families, and have incorporated into their programs the various skills and services necessary to make a constructive contribution to both the child and the family. Other groups are more limited in their approach. Parents often use day care services without regard to their stated purpose. They see such supplemental care as a way of helping them bring up their children, and they expect it to provide for children's growth needs as well as providing protection.

Just as today's family should be able to expect adequate health, education, and cultural facilities in the community, so should it be able to expect good supplemental day care facilities.

Day care services may be provided in a family setting or in a group (such as a day care center or preschool), depending on which form is more appropriate for the child and the family situation. This guide is concerned only with group day care programs for young children. It is based on the assumption that wherever and whenever young children are brought together in groups for a part of the day, certain conditions must prevail if the experience is to be beneficial to the children and their parents. It is important, therefore, that we cut across the artificial lines of demarcation created by the different names given to group programs and the various auspices under which they operate. Instead, let us try to come to grips with the factors that make a day care center—under whatever name or auspices—a good place for young children to spend some of their hours each day.

Day Care Centers: An Overview

What Is a Day Care Center?

A day care center is a place where the preschool child has an opportunity to learn through play with other children and with appropriate toys and materials; where mental, emotional, and physical growth is fostered; and where nutritious food, health supervision, medical care, rest, and activity are provided as needed. All this is done by a staff specially trained in the care and development of the preschool child, and with educational toys and equipment specially designed to foster the child's growth. It is a place where parents, for some hours each day, can leave their children and thus share their care and upbringing with the staff of the center.

A day care center may also be a place where the school-age child goes for recreational activities and for the adult supervision he or she needs during some of the out-of-school hours. For a child of this age, too, growth needs are met by a staff trained to provide the amount of supervision and the types of activities appropriate to the child's age. Food, health supervision, and rest—as well as activities—are made available as needed. The day care center's program for the school-age child supplements both the home and the school.

A Child's Typical Day at a Day Care Center

Michael is four years old. He lives with his mother, father, older brother, and baby sister in a large apartment house not very far from the center. Michael's mother and sister usually accompany him to the center in the morning and call for him in the afternoon. When his sister is sick and his mother must stay with her, Michael's father takes him to the center much earlier than usual, and a neighbor brings him home. Sometimes Michael has to stay home because there is no one to take him and call for him. Then Michael is sad; he has to stay indoors all day and has no one to play with.

When Michael arrives at the center he goes right to his classroom. His teacher[1] greets him and looks him over to make sure he seems to be in good health. Whenever she can, Michael's mother takes time to stop and talk a few minutes with the teacher. Michael is anxious to greet his friends, so he waves good-by and goes to hang up his jacket on his own special hook identified with his name and a picture. Michael cannot read yet, but the picture of a dinosaur tells him that this is his hook.

Michael quickly finds his special friends—Sarah, who always comes earlier than he does because her mother goes to work, and Shawn, whose father has to bring him to school early because his mother is sick. Michael greets the other teacher and has just time enough to put a puzzle together before his teacher announces that it is juice time.

Michael sits at a high table with other children and enjoys his apple juice and crackers. When they are finished, the teacher tells the children that it is time for them to choose something to do. Michael and two of his friends carefully make a large apartment house of blocks. When the building is almost completed, Sarah comes to ask Michael to be the "father" in the doll corner. Soon Michael is having "breakfast" with Sarah and two "babies"; then he takes his hat and goes off to "work," just like his own father. After a while, Michael goes over to the easel, paints a large, colorful picture, and asks the teacher to hang it on the wall. Then it is cleanup time; all the children join the teachers in putting everything away neatly in its place and making the room tidy. When this is done, the children arrange their chairs around the teacher. She tells them a story about springtime and what it means, and teaches them a new song about the first flowers of spring.

Now it is time for outdoor play. Michael and his classmates troop to the large play yard, and soon Michael is busy climbing and swinging. Later, with the outdoor blocks, he builds a large garage for the wagon.

---

[1] Throughout this volume *teacher* is used to refer to both the fully qualified teacher and the assistants providing direct care to the child.

When the children come inside, one of their teachers reads them a story about a boy who takes a walk in the country. The children act out the story, and Michael has a turn pretending to be that boy. Then Michael quickly washes his hands to help the teacher set the tables for lunch. After lunch is on the table, Michael joins his friends in eating a tasty hot meal. The teacher is eating at Michael's table today, and all the children enjoy talking to her and to each other while they eat. When most of the children have finished, the teacher tells them they may be excused to wash up and get ready for a nap. The teacher stays at the table a little longer with the new boy, a slow eater. The children take off their shoes (except for the new boy, who doesn't want to) and curl up under blankets on their cots. The teacher sings a naptime song, and soon Michael is fast asleep.

After his nap, Michael has a glass of milk and a cookie. The teacher brings out the drums, bells, and tambourines, and Michael has a chance to play a drum in the orchestra. Then the children put on their jackets, some to go outdoors to play, because they stay later in the day, and others, like Michael, to get ready to leave. About this time Michael's mother arrives. Michael takes his painting home to show his family, says good-bye to his teacher and classmates, and leaves happily, telling his mother all about his busy day. He can hardly wait for tomorrow, when his group will visit the firehouse.

The children who remain at school longer play outdoors for a while, then come indoors, wash up, and play quiet games or listen to stories until their parents call for them. If they have to stay very late in the day, they may even have another snack and perhaps another rest on their cots.

How the Day Care Center Helps Meet the Child's Needs

Children have certain basic needs and certain characteristics common to all children on their age level. But each child is also an individual with his or her own unique characteristics, needs, and family environment. A good day care center establishes its program to provide for the basic growth needs of every young child, and, at the same time, takes into consideration the needs of the individual child and family. With such a program, not only will each child have a safe, wholesome, enriching environment, but those who require more care and protection will also have their special needs met.

Every child has certain needs for growth and development, and a good day care center can help parents to meet them. Some of these needs are:

The security of family life. The center is a place where parents or surrogate parents can leave the child for some hours each day, with the assurance that the child is having a safe, wholesome, happy time. The parents know that the staff understands their needs as well as the child's.

Protection from hazards to health and safety. Responsible, capable teachers and other staff members see to it that the children are protected from danger and that their needs for rest, exercise, good nutrition, and safe behavior are being met.

Protection from disease and promotion of good health. Health supervision and medical care referrals are provided as needed.

Nutritionally balanced diet. Balanced meals and snacks are provided in the amounts children require, according to the time each child spends at the day care center.

Exercise. Opportunity is offered each day for active play indoors and out, with equipment that is specially designed to develop the child's body.

Rest. There is a balance between quiet and active play, and time to rest or nap.

Love and self-confidence. Day care centers have teachers who love children, who know how to give a child recognition and a sense of individual worth, and who know the importance of a child's relationship to the family and how to maintain and strengthen it.

Companions and friends. The child has the opportunity to play with other children of similar age and interests under the guidance of teachers who know how to make certain that these experiences will be pleasant and friendly.

Social behavior. The center provides the child with the experience of being a member of a group under the guidance of trained teachers who know how to help the child develop self-control. At the same time that the children learn to stand up for their own rights, they learn to take turns, to share, to consider others' rights and feelings, and to give up some of their individual rights for the greater good of the group.

Some independence. The children learn how to help themselves, to solve problems appropriate to their ages, and to make some decisions about their own behavior.

Intellectual stimulation. The children have an opportunity to become acquainted with the world through stories, songs, pictures, trips, and firsthand contacts with a variety of materials and educational toys under the guidance of teachers who know how to help them learn from these experiences.

Skills. The day care center helps the child develop language facility and competence.

Creative experiences. The children are given the chance to express their feelings and ideas through the use of raw materials such as clay, paints, and blocks; through dramatic play; and through experiences with language and music.

Because the growth stages of the preschool child are interrelated, every group program must be prepared to meet all these needs in an integrated fashion.

We cannot give the child food this week, social experience next week, and education the week after. Children grow and learn in all aspects of their beings at the same time. To withhold the conditions children need for normal growth in any aspect—physical, social, emotional, or mental— is to restrict their development in some way. Sick or undernourished children are not ready for sustained mental stimulation, nor can they engage in the vigorous exercise they need for physical development. Children deprived of the feeling of being loved cannot develop normal relationships with others, nor can they give their attention to learning if they are preoccupied with an unsatisfied need for affection and attention. Day care centers base their programs on this knowledge; they know that contributing to the all-round development of the child is their principal job.

Depending on the individual child, the family background, and other relationships, the day care center will play a greater or lesser part in the child's growth and development during every 24-hour day. It is of the greatest importance that the staff of the day care center have a profound knowledge of the essentials for healthy, normal growth of the young child. When the day care center enters into partnership with the child's family, it obligates itself to meet the child's care and development needs to the degree necessary for supplementing the family's care.

The day care center may be meeting other needs, too. These may be the needs of working parents for a safe, wholesome place to leave their children during the day; of overburdened parents, particularly parents of children with special needs, for some relief from the tasks of child care; of chemically dependent parents or parents at risk of child abuse who are participating in rehabilitation programs; of parents who need to complete school or job training programs; of parents who work at night and must sleep during the day; and of all parents for guidance in understanding how children grow and learn, and how to handle normal behavior and incipient behavior problems.

The individual child's needs cannot be met without also considering what is good for his or her family. A paramount objective of any day care center, however, must be its positive contribution to the healthy growth and development of the child. Sometimes it is necessary for children to be in the day care center more hours each day than their need for group activity requires. But when the family situation calls for such extended supplementary care, the experience in the day care center can still be made a wholesome and happy one if the program is geared to meeting the needs of children and families.

Licensing: The Community's Part in Safeguarding the Well-Being of Children at the Center

No matter under what auspices or for which stated purposes the day care center operates, the community has a responsibility for safeguarding the well-being of the children attending the center. Providing a service for young children is a serious matter. If the center's building is not safe; if the personnel are irresponsible, indifferent, or abusive; or if the daily program is inappropriate, the children can be harmed rather than helped. A day care center must be more than merely a place to keep the child safe, more than just a building filled with attractive toys. Its staff must have a concept of child development and a program that will give children the things they need for healthy growth.

The best way to be sure of safeguarding children while they are away from their parents is to have a strong licensing law applicable to every individual, group of individuals, organization, or institution that cares for children in groups during any hours of the day. Almost all communities require licenses for restaurants, beauty parlors, barber shops, pet shops, and so on, to assure minimal health protection. Where the young children of our community are concerned, this protection is particularly important, because the health and the psychological development of the children are both at stake.

Licensing standards for day care centers should cover the following elements:

Building and fire safety—proper accident protection, sanitation, water supply, sewage disposal

Enrollment—number and ages of children to be accepted in relation to staff and space available

Staff—size, type, and training necessary, and provision for criminal background and child abuse registry record checks

Health measures to protect the group and the individual child—including immunization, disease control, and HIV/AIDS policy and practice guidelines[2]

Furnishings, supplies, and equipment

Licensing alone cannot guarantee the best care for each individual child, but it can provide minimum standards for child care practice. When the licensing agency employs or otherwise makes available staff members trained in early childhood education, health, and social work to interpret the standards and to help day care centers meet them, the licensing program becomes a constructive force for improving the quality of center programs.

To learn what the day care licensing law is in your community and what protection it provides for children, write to your state or local department of social services, welfare, health, or education; the licensing authority is usually vested in one of these four governmental agencies. Generally, the department with licensing authority has a cooperative arrangement with other departments to assure to children in day care centers the best protection possible in such areas as safety, sanitation, nutrition, and health, and at least some of the things necessary for their social, mental, and emotional growth and development. Unfortunately, some state laws exempt certain types of centers from licensing requirements.

When the licensing law is not sufficiently comprehensive to give full protection, the community can do something about it, if enough people care about the well-being of children. The legislature or city council can be urged to pass a new day-care-center licensing law. A committee of parents and child development professionals can be formed to make

---

[2] See *Guidelines for Serving Children with AIDS in Child Day Care* (Washington, DC: Child Welfare League of America), 1992.

recommendations on standards for licensing and to interpret to the public the importance of such standards.[3]

Sometimes, in the absence of adequate licensing regulations, the community can raise standards through consultation and advocacy offered by a parents committee, a community-based providers group, a resource and referral agency, or a private or public agency that employs experts in day care service. The helpfulness of such consultation services depends, of course, on how well they are used. But most people who care for young children want to do a good job; their failure to do so is usually due to lack of knowledge rather than to ill will or indifference. When providers can get it, they appreciate advice and help with programing, staffing, administration, and other responsibilities.

Every community can call on experts from outside—either through state governmental agencies or through national public and private agencies and accreditation bodies concerned with day care. Even if the community has a large number of people who are experienced and qualified to direct day care programs, it is a good idea to bring in someone from the outside occasionally. This provides local programs with an objective evaluation and helps them to compare their standards with those in other communities and learn about new trends around the country.

---

[3] See *Standards of Excellence for Child Day Care Service* (Washington, DC: Child Welfare League of America), 1992.

Starting a Day Care Program

Who Operates Day Care Centers?

Day care centers may be operated by any of the following:

- A public institution or agency—a department of social services, recreation, education, or welfare; a hospital; or a branch of the armed forces

- A private institution or agency—a child welfare agency, a religious organization, a university, a hospital, a community center, or a private or voluntary family and children's agency

- An incorporated citizens' board of directors or an association

- A parent cooperative group

- An individual owner or a for-profit corporation

- A labor union

- An industry

- An employer of any type

What Does It Take to Start a Day Care Program?

Before you set up a day care program, certain requirements for its successful operation must be met:

1. A knowledge of what a day care center can do to help the development of the children who will attend it

2. An understanding of the needs of parents in your particular community for this kind of supplemental child care and of the needs of their children

3. A clearly formulated and agreed-upon statement of purposes

4. A business plan that includes estimates of all expenses for operating the program according to standards that will assure good care for the children

5. An assured source of funds to equal the estimated expenses

6. A knowledge of the legal requirements for operating a day care center in your community

7. Access to comprehensive liability insurance and information on critical risk management policies and procedures

8. An administrative body, which may be a department of a public or private agency, an incorporated board of directors, or an individual, and which will be responsible for financing, for establishing operating policies, for efficiently disbursing funds, and for maintaining high standards of care

9. Policies for admission of children

10. Policies for behavior management

11. Policies for employment of the staff

12. A building (or part of a building) that is safe and has adjacent outdoor play space and sufficient space for classrooms, a kitchen, food storage, toilet and handwashing facilities, offices, and storage of supplies and first-aid equipment

13. Equipment suitable for a day care center, such as small tables

and chairs, kitchen and lavatory furnishings and installations, office furnishings, cots or mats for resting, educational toys and materials, and outdoor playground apparatus

14. A program for the whole child that uses knowledge from the disciplines of early childhood education, health, nutrition, social work, and mental health to provide an experience suitable to the ages of the children and their individual needs

15. A staff professionally qualified to plan and carry out such an integrated program

16. Contacts with other community agencies, institutions, and resources to which families can be referred for services not supplied by the day care center, from which consultation services can be obtained as needed, and with which there can be community planning for children and parents

All of these factors are indispensable to the operation of a program that really serves children and their families well. If you are about to start a day care center, do not begin unless you are sure that you can fulfill each of the requirements noted above. If you are already operating a day care center, you are not serving the children well unless all these requirements are met. The chapters that follow give some suggestions for doing so.

How Are Day Care Centers Financed?

Good day care is expensive. It is not a cheap substitute for some other kind of care. Bringing up children is expensive—and the cost to the community and the family will be even greater in later years if young children are shortchanged. The right kind of day care program at the right time in a child's life will, in the long run, prove to be economical. When a community holds this conviction, adequate financing can usually be found.

Funds to operate a day care center can be obtained from a number of sources:

- Payment of fees by parents

- Public funds from local, state, or federal governmental agencies

- Businesses and employers

- Voluntary contributions to local joint fund-raising campaigns

- Voluntary contributions to individual agency fund-raising campaigns

- Endowments

- Special gifts

- Special funds for research and demonstration

A day care center may be financed by money from one source only, or, as is more often the case, by combined funds from several sources. Community support depends on interpretation of the program's benefits and its importance as a possible means of preventing much greater costs in money and quality of life in later years.

Parents' Fees

Several factors are involved in payment of fees by parents whose children attend a day care center: family income, the auspices of the center, available financing, and community willingness to assist working parents. Fees also reflect the reality that significant public funding for day care programs is only beginning to become available. Because good day care is expensive, and because programs provided entirely under public or philanthropic auspices can no longer meet the demand for child care in most communities, parents' fees must usually be counted on to meet a share of the costs.

Voluntary centers without philanthropic endowments and with only partial public subsidies must collect the remainder of the actual cost of operation from the parents, frequently on a sliding fee scale. Individual or corporate for-profit proprietors must collect the actual cost of operation and also make a profit (a modest one, it is hoped). In parent-cooperative centers, the fees equal the actual costs. It is encouraging that scholarships are increasingly being made available by day care centers operating under many different auspices.

In all communities there are some parents who can pay the required fee and who are sufficiently aware of the value of day care to be willing to do so. Other parents, such as working single parents, may pay at a sacrifice because no other resource is available. But the majority of families cannot meet the full cost of a good day care program, no matter how urgently they want it or need it.

Community-based not-for-profit agencies have based policy on the belief that when parents share the cost of day care, they have a heightened sense of involvement in the care of their children. Whether parents really do feel better and more responsible when they pay for day care will not be debated here, nor shall we discuss whether the practice of collecting fees and the inconsistencies among publicly supported programs on this matter reflect community attitudes toward low-income families. The present reality is that not enough funds are available from all sources combined to meet the need for various kinds of day care programs. If the available funds are to be stretched as much as possible, parents' contributions are necessary. This is, however, a matter all communities must examine as more funds become available and as communities recognize the importance of day care. Are children to be deprived of day care because their parents cannot or will not pay for it?

In today's not-for-profit and publicly supported centers, a sliding fee scale usually determines parents' contributions. The scale is based on two factors: (1) the actual annual cost of operation, divided by the number of children enrolled, and (2) the level of income in a given community below which a family cannot maintain itself adequately. Fees are graduated from no payment for families having an income below the established minimum level for the community up to the maximum, which would be the center's actual cost per child. Consideration is thus given to each family situation, including net income and number of family members. When a sliding scale is used, fees should always accord with the actual family situation and should be adjusted upward or downward as that situation changes.

Since the cost of operating the center remains the same whether or not an individual child is present on a given day, there is no logical reason for reducing or waiving fees in relation to absences. The regular fee should be charged in order to hold the child's place, and many agencies have adopted this policy. Adjustments in fees should be made, however, if the family income has been lowered or if unusual family expenses have been incurred during the child's absence.

Public Funds

Public funds (monies allocated for day care programs through governmental agencies) usually have certain limitations on their use. Early childhood development is still not universally recognized as an integral part of a child's total education and development, so public day care money may be available only for children of single working parents, of low-income families, of culturally deprived backgrounds, of migrant workers, or of some other limited category.

Sometimes the entire program is supported by public funds and operated by public agencies. More often, public money is made available to private for-profit and not-for-profit agencies to provide day care services on the basis of publicly established eligibility criteria and program standards. Public funds can also be spent on a purchase-of-service or voucher basis for children cared for by community-based not-for-profit agencies or commercially operated centers that meet certain eligibility requirements and standards of care.

Specific contributions, such as surplus foods, free and reduced cost meals and snacks under the Department of Agriculture Food and Nutrition Service Child Care Food Program, and medical care, are often made available to day care programs by governmental agencies. In many communities local housing authorities provide space for day care centers at prevailing economic rentals or on a rent-free basis, as an in-kind contribution to the local share of antipoverty Community Action Programs. Also, in many communities, the local housing authority finances needed facilities for centers jointly with local agencies. In some instances, permission to erect a separate building on public-housing grounds has been granted to a sponsoring agency.

Public funding is also available to working parents through the Dependent Care Tax Credit, and, in some instances, employers may provide access to additional child care tax options through dependent care assistance programs, and/or claim state or federal tax advantages in relation to provision of child care services for their employees.

Businesses and Employers

Employers are a small but growing source of funding for day care services, particularly employers in service industries such as hospitals that require a stable work force. Options for employer-assisted child care include: on-site or near-site centers; purchase of day care slots in local day care centers for employees; contributions of money or resources to community-based programs; and employer-based dependent care assistance plans such as cafeteria benefit plans and flexible spending accounts that facilitate use of nontaxable dollars for employees' child care expenses.

Local Joint Fund-Raising Campaigns

In many communities, all privately financed philanthropic agencies join in one annual campaign for public support. To share in funds raised by such an appeal, agencies must meet a community need and must operate on a not-for-profit basis; they are usually also required to be incorporated according to state laws and to give satisfactory evidence of meeting standards for the type of program they offer.

Funds raised in a joint campaign are designed to make up the difference between an agency's expected income from all other sources and its estimated annual expenses. The goal of a joint campaign is based on the combined needs of all member agencies. Depending on the success of the drive, funds are allocated to the agencies in proportion to approved budget requests. In some communities the joint fund-raising campaign is directed to a limited group of people, and participating agencies can expect to receive only a limited share of their budgets from this source.

Joint fund-raising campaigns generally do not provide money for the purchase or construction of buildings. Agencies that need money for these purposes must get it from other sources—gifts, special fund-raising drives, or their own capital funds.

An unfortunate practice often found in the allocation of funds from both the joint fund-raising campaign and the public agency is reimbursement for days of pupil attendance rather than an outright allocation that represents a certain share or percentage of the annual budget. The system of attendance reimbursement is based on a false premise. All expenses continue whether the child is present or not, and the child's place must be held open, at least for the period that absence is due to a reasonable cause, such as illness or family travel. When a day care center is dependent on a maximum attendance every day to meet its ongoing expenses, it is tempted to over-enroll, perhaps to the point of danger, and thus to lower standards. This policy may even lead to allowing a sick child to remain in the group in order to keep income at the necessary level. Total enrollment is a more realistic basis for allocating funds, with the requirement that the rolls be kept active and vacancies promptly filled.

Individual Agency Fund-Raising Campaigns

Annual membership dues, written appeals at certain times of the year, theater benefits, thrift shops, fairs, sports events, or any of a number of other activities may be used by an agency to raise money. Some long-established agencies, well known for the quality of their programs and their importance to children in the community, have sufficient experience in this type of fund-raising to estimate fairly accurately how much they can raise. Others have found individual fund-raising campaigns a precarious method of financing, particularly if the campaigns represent their only source of funds.

Endowments

Endowment funds are an important source of income, and agencies should seek new bequests. Agency boards must give careful attention to keeping investments as sound as possible.

A few day care centers are fortunate enough to have a continuing and assured income from endowments or property belonging to the corporate body. In the past, this enabled some agencies to meet almost their entire operating costs. As costs rise, however, income from investments alone is usually not sufficient.

Special Gifts

One-time grants may be given by a foundation, by an individual for specific purposes, or in memory of someone previously associated with the day care center.

Research and Demonstration Funds

Funds for research and demonstration of a new aspect of day care center programming may sometimes be obtained for a limited time. Unless the center has been specifically established for the purpose of research and demonstration, such funds will be allocated only for the staff and equipment necessary to carry out the project and cannot be used to defray normal, ongoing operating costs. The money may enrich or augment the program, but it will not take care of budget deficits.

What Are the Costs
of Operating a Center?

Once it has been decided to set up a day care center, adequate financing must be found. The budget items set forth in the following pages are for a program without frills, and represent realistic ongoing annual expenses.

- Salaries and employee benefits (for all categories of staff members—professionals, support personnel, and consultants)

- Insurance

- Rent (if applicable)

- Building repairs

- Utilities—electricity, gas, water, heat, air conditioning

- Household supplies

- Household equipment (repair and replacement)

- Food

- Educational equipment (repair and replacement)

- Educational supplies

- Office supplies

- Postage and telephone

- Publicity, auditing, staff training and development

- Purchased services

- Transportation (if provided by the center)

Salaries and Employee Benefits

It often comes as a shock to donors to philanthropic agencies, and sometimes even to board members, to learn that salaries make up the biggest item in a center's budget. But day care is a highly labor intensive service, and staff is the key to the service. The program will be only as good as the staff that develops it and carries it out. There can be no economizing on staff—either in numbers or in quality of professional competence. Salary scales may vary from one community to another, but the proportion of salary expenses in the total budget is usually 80 percent or more. In our present mobile society, the community with a salary level lagging far behind the national average will soon find itself without qualified personnel; sometimes those same communities are the ones that must pay the most to lure back the professional people they need.

Salary estimates for budget purposes should include payments for social security and other agency retirement plans, unemployment insurance, workers compensation, medical and hospital insurance, and replacements for staff absences and for vacations if the day care center remains open on a year-round basis. The budget must also allow for normal salary increments according to the policy adopted by the agency.

Insurance

Insurance is an item sometimes neglected in making up a budget. It is, however, essential to the responsible operation of a day care program, and should be considered as part of administrative costs. Fluctuations in the liability insurance market make it important to investigate insurance costs and coverage thoroughly. Existing center operators, day care associations, and resource and referral agencies may be useful information sources. Architects and builders may be helpful with respect to property insurance. Consult local government agencies to learn which code requirements apply.

In general, insurance should include coverage for property (fire and theft); workers' compensation for staff members; public liability for children, staff members, parents and others while in or on the center's property; and transportation-related liability if the center is providing transportation daily or for field trips. Other forms of insurance may be available and advisable under certain circumstances.

Installation Expenses

When a day care center opens, a special budget for start-up will be required. If the building is being converted, money must be allotted for appropriate kitchen and bathroom facilities, protection for windows and stairways, fencing around the play yard, perhaps floor covering for the classrooms, and equipment and furnishings of all types. There may also be an architect's fee. Estimates for building alterations or construction should be obtained from local contractors. Estimates on educational equipment and supplies can be obtained from catalogs of educational equipment companies. The social services, health, education, and welfare departments in the state may also have helpful information on costs involved in setting up a day care center.

Contributions in Kind: Imputed Costs

When contributions are made—as is often the case—in the form of rent, food, equipment, medical and nursing care, or casework services, they should be given a monetary value and included in computing overall costs, even though they are not counted as a part of the budget in setting fees or making requests to a public agency or the community fund-raising campaign. These contributions are all essential components of the program; every agency should be aware of what they cost and be prepared to find adequate financing should they be withdrawn or prove to be unsatisfactory as contributions.

Many budget items will vary from one community to another and according to the number of hours per day and weeks per year the center is open. Also, when infants, sick children, or children with handicaps or special needs are being cared for, some costs will be greater. A larger staff will be needed, including staff members with special skills. For children who have physical handicaps, expensive equipment of a special nature is often required.

Since so many factors are variable, it would be unrealistic to attempt here to give any per capita cost for day care.

Administering the Day Care Center

Whether the governing body of a new day care center is a public department, an incorporated board, an unincorporated group, or an individual, it must assume certain administrative functions in order to protect the children and discharge its responsibility to the parents. The governing body must:

- Assure adequate financing

- Employ a director who can be depended upon to plan, organize, and carry on the work of the day care center within established general policies and to lead in the formulation of center policies. The director must establish and maintain channels of communication with staff members at all levels so that the administration has access to the knowledge of the staff and the staff has an understanding of the purposes of the administration and the place of the day care center in the community

- Formulate policies for admission of children and employment of staff members

- Interpret to the community the center's work, its resources, and its needs

- Evaluate the present program in terms of standards for the field and the needs of the community

- Plan for the future

If the administrative body is an incorporated board of directors, it must also ascertain that:

- The articles of incorporation are in order and in line with the purposes and program of the center

- Board members are knowledgeable about the community the center serves, interested in the center's work, and able and willing to give time to the job of being board members

- Bylaws cover provisions for the election of new officers and board members at reasonable intervals; for regular meetings; for necessary and appropriate recording and reporting of meetings; for the appointment of committees with specific, delegated responsibilities pertinent to the center's purposes and program; and for the taking of necessary action in emergencies between board meetings or when a quorum is not present

Determining Admission Policies

Every organization offering a day care program must decide which children it will serve, on the basis of the following factors:

- The need of parents in the community for supplemental child care

- Which children a day care program can benefit and which children it cannot help

- The number and ages of children the center is prepared to care for, which in turn depend on the amount of money at the organization's disposal, the size and kind of premises available or to be built, local and state regulations, the type of program required by the children in the community, and the availability of staff members to carry on the program

In other words, every group day care program is good for some children but not for others. A day care program can be designed to meet a variety of needs or it can be limited to one or two specific needs. Even a public agency that may have a mandate to accept all requests for service does not have a mandate to provide the wrong service or a service that would be harmful to a particular child. Certain criteria for acceptance must obtain in all programs. Some communities feel that children of single parents in welfare job training programs, more than others, require this form of supplemental care, and give priority to this group. Others put ceilings on the family's income in deciding eligibility for philanthropically or publicly supported centers.

It seems unfortunate, however, in light of the benefits young children derive from the day care center experience, to set up restrictions that create categories and prevent the free association of children with others whose backgrounds are different from their own. All children should learn to know people from a wide variety of backgrounds. Where fiscally and geographically feasible, a socioeconomic mix of children and families is a highly desirable goal.

If they have the will (and the imagination and the resources), child day care professionals can plan a program to meet a wide variety of needs and give the right care for almost all children.

The primary criteria for eligibility, regardless of other factors, are first, the individual child's emotional readiness to be separated from the parent or parents,[4] even for a few hours a day, and second, the parents' readiness to share the care of their child with the staff of the day care center. These criteria can be determined only by an individual interview with the parents, who should visit the center with their child. These criteria must be considered apart from other factors of eligibility, if possible emotional damage to the child is to be avoided.[5]

Other essential criteria include the age and health of the child and the regularity of her or his attendance.

Age

Group day care is clearly beneficial for most children between three and six years of age, and for children from six to 12 who need care during their out-of-school hours. Because of the substantial increase in parents' need to work, however, some form of day care for infants and toddlers has also become a critical necessity for a growing number of families. Research continues to evaluate this type of care. It is too soon to know for certain under what conditions infants can be cared for in groups without damage to their development. For the present, family day care is considered the best supplementary care resource for infants.

---

[4] *Parent*, as used throughout this guide, includes foster parents and other responsible caregivers.

[5] See "Relationships between Parents and Day Care Center Staff," p. 89.

Very young children are generally not ready for group living. They need a highly personalized individual relationship with an adult, and can suffer if they do not have it. Some two-year-olds—but not all—are ready for limited hours of group activity. They require small groups and very special programming to make day care a worthwhile experience. Centers serving toddlers and twos must have a high ratio of staff to children and strictly limit the size of groups.

Health

Children admitted to the center should pass a physical examination that indicates their status with respect to communicable disease and mental or physical handicaps that would prevent their participation in group activities or expose them to physical or psychological damage.

Since HIV infection cannot be identified in very young children, and discrimination against children or employees who may have been exposed to the virus is both unethical and, under provisions of the federal government and most states, illegal, universal health care precautions must be standard practice in all child day care centers. For information on this and other topics related to HIV and day care, see *Serving Children with HIV Infection in Child Day Care* [CWLA 1991].

Research and experience have demonstrated that many children with handicaps can benefit from group experience with other children who do not have handicaps. This depends, however, on the nature of the handicap, and the staff, the program, and the physical plant and equipment available. Children with serious mental retardation need a special training program; they can become unhappy and frustrated if forced to try to keep up with other youngsters of their own age. Children with serious physical handicaps need special equipment, special premises, and specially trained staff. Children with serious emotional problems also need special staff and special conditions. Including children with special needs in a group program requires careful diagnosis and analysis, along with constant evaluation of their progress and their effect on the group (and vice versa).

A child with a handicap may be able to participate in a group program if the program is specially organized to meet his or her needs; in fact, such programs have been found to be a highly effective form of treatment.

Regular Attendance

Children can benefit from the opportunities offered by a group day care program only if they attend regularly. One of the important developmental opportunities offered in a group experience is the chance to develop relationships to other children. If a child is absent frequently, he or she may feel strange and unacquainted with the other children. During the one child's absence, the others will be forming friendships, learning how to play together, and acquiring new skills and knowledge. Children who attend irregularly may feel like outsiders and may not be able to keep up with the play or conversation of the other children because they have not shared the other children's experiences.

A day care center is not intended to be used only for short periods of time at the parents' convenience, nor for emergencies in lieu of a respite service. A good center has an ongoing, evolving program in which children have to be fully participating members if they are to reap its benefits.

These are basic considerations in determining admissions. Once the center's administrative body decides whether it wants to meet one special category of need or many within the same program, it can set up appropriate admission requirements.

Personnel Policies and Practices

Every day care center, big or small, public or private, must have rules to regulate the work of the staff, or chaos will reign. Staff members should know what their responsibilities are; what resources, benefits, and privileges are available to them; and what they will be paid, when, why, and how. They should understand their relationships to other staff members and know to whom they are responsible. They should be able to bring their needs and suggestions to the attention of someone who can do something about them. And, most important, the staff must understand the purpose of the program and how each member fits into it.

The best way to decide on staff policies and procedures is for staff representatives to participate in program and policy development with the administration. Since it is the responsibility of the latter to see that these policies are carried out, however, final approval must be given by the administration. Obviously, at times it will be necessary to compromise between what the staff thinks is just—and even essential—and what the administration knows is realistic in terms of finances, work schedules, or procedures that directly affect the welfare of the children. But the more the administration and the staff exchange opinions and ideas, the more they examine each other's points of view, the greater will be the mutual agreement and sharing of goals.

Even in the smallest, simplest organization, personnel policies and practices should be in writing, available to all members of the staff and the

governing body.[6] Everyone working in the organization should understand:

- The purpose of the agency

- Employment procedures (references, physical examinations,
  contracts, probationary periods [if any], and tenure of employment)

- Job definitions

- Qualifications for each staff position

- Hours of work

- Policies on sick leave, vacations, leaves of absence, holidays

- Employee benefits—health, medical, workers' compensation,
  and other insurance plans; social security; pension plans; and
  child care and training opportunities

- Procedures for periodic evaluation of performance, and for
  resignation and dismissal

- Plans for staff development, conference attendance, and educational leave

- Responsibilities for attendance at staff meetings and parent
  meetings and participation in committees of the staff and the
  governing body

Job Classifications and Salaries

Necessary corollaries to this set of personnel practices are job
classifications and salary ranges for all position classifications. These also
should be in writing and available to both the staff and the governing
body. Sometimes administrators think that staff members will be happier
with their salaries if they do not know what anyone else is being paid. This
is a mistaken attitude that can undermine morale and lead to a disastrous

[6] See *Preparing a Personnel Policy Manual* (Washington, DC: Child Welfare League of
America), 1991.

staff turnover level. It is only human for all staff members to be interested in knowing how the salary for one position compares with that for another. For every position in the agency, there should be:

- A statement of minimum qualifications

- A salary range, from a stated minimum to a stated maximum

- A plan for fitting new staff members into the scale according to their qualifications

- A plan for increments, with their amount and frequency

The personnel practices should also include the following:

- A statement of any plan for upgrading staff members, on the basis of either improved qualifications or increased responsibility

- A statement of provision for periodic review of salary scales and a plan for staff participation in the review

Salaries and personnel practices have to be competitive with other community organizations that employ the same type of personnel. It is unrealistic to expect that because a day care center may be financed by charitable contributions, the staff should work for salaries below the going rate for their qualifications.

The work of the day care center will be only as good as the personnel it employs. Good personnel policies and salary scales are an essential means of assuring that qualified people will join the staff and stay.

Housing the Day Care Center

The building or space in which the day care center is located is not as important as what goes on inside. Depending on whether the staff knows its job or not, good programs can be found in makeshift quarters and poor programs in luxurious, modern buildings. If economy is necessary, it is better to economize on the building than on the staff.

Although the center's quarters need not be luxurious, certain requirements of space and facilities are essential for the comfort and safety of young children and for the activities associated with a day care center program.

Location of the Center

Optimally, the premises of a day care center should be within walking distance of the homes of the children who will attend it. It is comforting to young children to have their "school" in their own neighborhood, among familiar surroundings. Long trips by bus or other transportation are fatiguing for small children and increase their exposure to contagious or infectious illnesses. Also, when parents do not accompany their children to the day care center, much of the important contact between the home and the center's staff is lost.

When the center is located in a residential neighborhood, it can have an influence on the community and maintain close contacts with it. Parents and staff members from local schools and other community agencies can see the building, watch the children come and go, and visit the center often. From this standpoint, public housing offers an excellent situation.

Exceptions to the rule of neighborhood-based day care centers may, of course, have to be made for very small or rural communities where one or two centers must serve children living in a wide geographic area. But even in such cases, it is best to avoid locating the center on a main street or a main highway. Sometimes, if transportation to the center is not provided, the building may have to be near available public transportation.

There is a growing trend toward situating day care centers in or near the plants or offices where parents work. Once this was not recommended, because it is difficult to assure safety for children in a commercial building or area, but the practice is becoming more acceptable as employers find ways to provide suitable environments near the workplace.

Caution: Know the local zoning ordinances before setting your heart on a particular location for your day care center.

Choosing a Building

The ideal day care center is in its own one-story building, specially designed for the purpose, and surrounded by outdoor play space. This arrangement is most suitable because:

- A small separate building can be given a homelike atmosphere, a great aid to the child in making the transition from home to the day care center.

- It is safe. There are no hazards from stairs and open stairwells, and no danger of falls from upper-story windows. In the event of fire or other emergencies, the building can be quickly and safely evacuated.

- It provides maximum security in terms of supervision, with no places for the children to wander off to and get lost. All staff members are easily within call of each other at all times.

- It eliminates unnecessary fatigue for the children and the staff.

- It is easily accessible to the handicapped.

- It permits children to have independence of movement with a minimum of regimentation.

- It permits maximum use of the outdoor play space.

- It permits planning activities according to what is best for the children rather than what is permitted within the building or what will not interfere with other occupants' schedules.

Next best to a separate building are quarters especially designed for the center on the main floor of an apartment building, a community center, a school, a place of worship, or some other existing structure. When such quarters are constructed as a separate unit with a private entrance and no overlapping use of space with other building occupants, they have most of the advantages of a separate building and, in some cases, certain added ones as well. For example, they may be more economical to maintain. And to the young child who lives in an apartment house, the center in such a building seems more like "home" than it would in any other setting.

Spacious private houses can sometimes be converted into very pleasant and homelike facilities for day care centers. Alterations and installations to make the place safe and suitable, however, are usually costly.

Sometimes a barracks-type building makes a simple, low cost, suitable day care center. Manufacturers of prefabricated buildings have shown an interest in designing structures of this type. Such buildings can house centers in communities where they may be needed temporarily or where urban redevelopment plans will be affecting the character of the neighborhood within a few years.

When day care staff and children must share space with other occupants of a multifunction building, problems are bound to arise. The center's program requires a different time schedule, different equipment, and a different arrangement and use of space than that of a business, a religious organization, or any other type of service. When several groups share the same facilities, additional labor is needed to remove and replace equipment for the center's various programs and to maintain the standard of cleanliness needed for the care of young children. Also, the noise and commotion in a building used by several groups are disturbing to young children, and in turn, their normal activity may be disturbing to older groups.

Climate and zoning laws must also be considered in determining the type of structure to select for the day care center.

Size of the Center

No one has yet decreed the optimal size for a day care center. At present, day care centers come in all sizes, from small, one-classroom units of 15 to 20 children to large centers serving over 100. During World War II some centers cared for several hundred children in large compounds especially built for the purpose. We are beginning to understand that the size of the center does not automatically effect economies of scale. Staff, equipment, and space must be increased in direct proportion to the number of children served. Although larger operations offer greater economies in the purchase of food, supplies, and equipment, and up to a certain point, in administrative cost per capita, beyond a certain point administrative and supervisory staff must be increased.

The young child responds best to a warm, homelike atmosphere, and is often confused or even frightened by bigness, whether in buildings or in crowds of people (including crowds of children). A center that serves a large number of children has to be big in size, and, no matter how carefully the space is designed for comfort and function, it still looks big to a small child. Although children spend the day with their own small group, they may be overwhelmed by the number of children they see at the hours of arrival and departure. This is the reason it is so important that the day care center quartered in a multifunction building have its own private entrance.

Most day care experts have found from experience that extremely large day care centers not only make it difficult to provide the proper surroundings for the young child, but are also difficult to administer. A day care center for from 50 to 100 children seems to be the preferred size, both for economy and ease of administration. In a center of this size, it is still possible to retain the homelike atmosphere children need. When a communitywide program is being planned, several small day care centers located near the children's homes should be the aim rather than one or two large, centrally located centers.

Space—How Much and What Kind?

A day care center building should be large enough to provide sufficient room for the children, the staff, and all program activities. How the space is divided and the size and location of the rooms have much to do with how well the staff can carry out an appropriate program and protect the children.

Where licensing regulations are in effect, there are specific minimal requirements for size and type of space in direct relation to the number and age of the children attending the center. These vary from one state or city to another. Whether legally required or not, the space allocations described in this guide are necessary for the efficient operation of a day care center.

Classrooms and Playrooms

1. Classrooms must have sufficient space for the children to move and play actively. Young children cannot and should not be required to sit still for long periods, as are older children in a regular school program. Classrooms should also be large enough to hold the necessary furnishings—tables, chairs, educational equipment, toys, and storage space for supplies.

2. An appropriate program for young children cannot be carried on with less than 50 square feet of classroom space per child, exclusive of toilet facilities, coatroom or lockers, and halls, especially if the classroom is used for the children's naps. Some licensing regulations require as much as three feet of space between cots.

3. A separate classroom should be permanently assigned for each group of children. This becomes their "home" at the center.

4. The number of children in a group should be determined both by the standards of national and state organizations for grouping children of each age and by the amount of space available. In other words, 50 young children cannot be placed in one group just because there is a room large enough to hold them. Nor can 15 children be put in a room that can hold only 10, just because the standards recommend 15 children in a group.

5. If a new day care center is being constructed, determine the number of children in each group and build classrooms according to the space requirements in item two above.

6. If an old building is to be converted and it does not have rooms that are large enough to accommodate groups of 12 to 20 children, the building is probably not suitable, unless a program is planned for children with very special needs who require smaller groups.

7. A classroom can be too big. Auditoriums, assembly halls, and other large spaces do not make suitable classrooms. Their size is frightening to many young children and overly exciting to others.

8. Whenever possible, classrooms should open directly onto the outdoor play space.

9. A low, flat-bottomed sink with running water for each classroom is a great asset.

10. A classroom should never be located completely below ground level.

Coatroom Space

1. *For children.* Preferably, specially designed individual private storage spaces should be placed in the hall close to the children's classroom, or in the classroom itself if the room is large enough. In any case, the space should be arranged so that each child's clothing is hung on a separate hook, has ventilation, and is easily accessible to the child.

2. *For staff.* Coatroom space should be convenient to that part of the building in which the staff members spend the major part of their time. For teachers, especially, it should be close to the classrooms so that outer clothing can be obtained quickly when it is time for outdoor activities.

3. *For parents and visitors.* Some space should be made available adjacent to the reception area.

Toilet and Handwashing Facilities

1. *For children.* An adequate number of toilets is particularly important in any place where young children are being cared for, and their accessibility is as important as their number. It is better to have several small toilet installations scattered throughout the building than one large central installation. In allocating toilet space, the area required for even a small installation

must be borne in mind. The *CWLA Standards of Excellence for Child Day Care Service* [CWLA 1992] specifies a ratio of one toilet for every ten children. But no matter how small the group of children, there should always be no fewer than two toilets available. The ideal arrangement is to have the toilet and handwashing rooms open directly off the playrooms. Where building structure permits, one toilet room with the right number of fixtures located between two classrooms can serve both groups. This arrangement is usually economical in installation, maintenance, and cost. If toilets cannot be adjacent to the classroom, they should at least be on the same floor. Toilet facilities are also needed adjacent to the outdoor play area.

2. *For staff.* Staff members must have toilet and washing facilities separate from those used by the children. If the staff is a large one, several washrooms will be needed. Where possible, they should be located conveniently throughout the building, that is, one near the teachers' rest area and one near the reception area.

Kitchen Facilities

A center that provides a hot meal needs a full-scale kitchen large enough to accommodate the type of equipment and the number of people required for preparing, cooking, and serving. Even when no hot meal is offered, the center should at least have a refrigerator and an area where wholesome snack foods can be stored and prepared.

Although a homelike atmosphere in the day care center is always emphasized, this cannot be carried over into the kitchen. Cooking for large groups is quite different from cooking for a family, and this fact must be recognized in planning space for food service.

The kitchen facilities should have several areas to allow for

- Receiving, checking, and storing foodstuffs and supplies

- Food preparation

- Garbage disposal

- Dishwashing and storage of dishes and utensils

- Serving of food

The kitchen should be located away from the classrooms, but not so far away that food gets cold while being served or that transporting food becomes difficult. Preferably, the kitchen should be on the ground floor, accessible to an outside entrance for ease of deliveries. If the classrooms are on an upper floor, however, it may be more convenient to have the kitchen there also, fire and building laws permitting.

The kitchen should be used exclusively for those things concerned with food preparation. Laundry, care of cleaning equipment, and so on should be done in another part of the building.

Utility Room

A high standard of cleanliness is essential in a day care center. Maintaining this standard requires planning for cleaning activities as an ongoing part of the operation.

One room, containing a sink with hot and cold water, should be allocated for the storage and care of cleaning equipment and for maintenance repairs. If laundry is done on the premises, the same room can also serve as the laundry. The utility room must always be separate from the kitchen.

Dining Area

No space is needed for a separate dining area. In most day care centers today, children eat in their own classrooms. It has been found that young children eat best in small groups, with their own teachers/caregivers and in familiar surroundings, at the same tables used for play activities earlier in the day. Food is brought to the classroom in covered casseroles and served by the teachers. Not only is this system better for the children, but it also saves space and equipment.

Napping Space

Preschool children at the day care center for more than a half day need a nap—or at least a resting period—with their bodies stretched out comfortably on cots or in sleeping bags. In most centers, the children sleep in their own classrooms. As with eating, the small group and the familiar surroundings create a calm atmosphere.

The classroom should be large enough to accommodate cots with an appropriate distance between them, although tables, chairs, and large indoor equipment may have to be moved to one side of the room or stacked. (A few centers still have the luxury of a separate room for napping. Although this arrangement makes less work for staff members, and provides a faster transition from lunch to naptime, it is not necessary, and may not be the best arrangement for the children.)

Private Space

Every center needs a room to keep children who become ill during the day away from the group until their parents call for them. The private space should be so located that a staff member will always be within sight and sound of the children and can keep them from feeling lonely. The room should also be not too far from the toilet facilities.

Medical and First-Aid Rooms

When physical examinations, medical treatment, or vaccinations and immunizations are given at the center, an appropriately equipped medical room is necessary. Sometimes this can be the same room that is used for private space. If it is, all supplies and equipment should be securely locked up, out of reach of the children. First-aid supplies, a necessity for every day care center, can also be kept in this room, securely locked up.

Areas for Adults

Although the day care center is concerned primarily with the well-being of children, the adults who care for them need certain facilities to do their job well.

Privacy is often difficult to achieve in a day care center. Most people tend to think of a center's program only in terms of what goes on in the classroom. But the program also involves continuing relationships among parents and staff. These call for a comfortable place where parents can be received, where they can meet in groups, and where they can talk privately with the teacher, the social worker, the director, the doctor, or the nurse.

The staff members, too, need space of their own, for conferences and for brief periods of rest. (The latter is especially important for the teachers, who are otherwise constantly with the children and usually engaged in some kind of physical activity.)

The administration of the center also requires its own space. Records must be kept, reports written, bills paid, supplies ordered, and so on.

The board of directors or other governing body of the center meets periodically. If these meetings can be held at the center, the directors will feel much closer to the program and the staff.

The amount of space to be allocated for these adult uses depends on the size of the center, on the number of staff members, and, to some extent, on the center's particular program. For example, if the center is used by a hospital or university for student internships, a room for the use of students may be necessary. If outside consultants (social workers, mental health personnel, doctors, nurses, etc.) are used regularly, they also may need some office space.

Minimally, every center should plan to include in its space for adults a reception area, one or more private offices, one or more rooms where staff members can rest, and at least one room where group meetings can be held.

Storage Space

For the children's safety, for convenience, and for good house-keeping, every center must have adequate storage space of the right kind and in the right places. The types of storage facilities depend upon the various materials and equipment to be stored and should be planned for before building alteration or construction is undertaken. Built-in storage space is best; otherwise, cupboards to hold supplies must be placed where necessary. It should be remembered, however, that cupboards in the classrooms reduce the area available for the children's activities.

Storage space is needed in the following places:

- Each classroom, for teachers' supplies currently in use

- The toilet rooms, for bathroom supplies currently in use

- The private space or medical room, for first-aid supplies

- The kitchen, for dishes, utensils, and perishable foods; near the kitchen, for reserve food stock

- The office, for office supplies

- The utility room, for cleaning supplies

- The playground (or adjacent to it), for storage of movable equipment

Centrally located storage space should be allocated for reserves of supplies bought in large quantities. Space is also needed to store an extra supply of clothing, seasonal play equipment, and toys awaiting repair.

Since one purpose of storage is to keep children away from things that may be dangerous for them or that should not be used without supervision, all storage spaces should have doors, locks, and keys.

Outdoor Play Space

All children need some outdoor play every day, except in the most inclement weather, not only for fresh air but also for a change of pace. Unless a center limits its program to as little as two half days a week, outdoor play space close at hand is necessary.

Sometimes, when children attend the center only for half days, a nearby public park may be used as a playground, but vigilant monitoring of its cleanliness and safety is imperative. Also, the type of outdoor play equipment that can be provided is sometimes limited. Another consideration is getting the children to and from the playground. Vacant lots in the neighborhood can be fixed up and used, but this, too, means transporting children and play equipment.

Children who come regularly to a day care center for more than a half-day session need their own playground, easily accessible and well equipped with appropriate materials and permanent installations for vigorous play.

Ideally, a playground should surround the building in such a way that each classroom opens directly onto it. If this is not feasible, it should at least adjoin the building. The playground should be adequate in size for the active play of the number of children in the center, taking into account that all the children do not have to be outdoors at the same time, particularly when the children range in age from the very young, such as toddlers, to school age.

In fact, it is preferable that not more than two classes share the playground at one time, and it is highly desirable that each group have some chance to use it alone. If the center is large, the playground may have to allow for two completely separate play areas so that two different age groups can play simultaneously. Approximately 200 square feet of playground space per child is recommended.

The following are factors to consider when planning a playground:

1. *Good drainage.* This makes it possible to use the playground after snowy or rainy weather.

2. *Several different kinds of surface covering, if possible.* There should be a hard surface for riding wagons and tricycles, dirt and sand for digging, and an area of grass—a delight to children and much safer for their active play than a hard surface.

3. *Sun and shade.* Trees provide the most pleasant shade, but if they are not available, awnings over some of the sunny areas can be substituted.

4. *Safety.* The playground surfaces and equipment, including the sandbox, should be checked daily and cleaned as often as necessary. All permanent equipment, such as slides, swings, and climbing apparatus, should be securely anchored. Equipment that moves, such as swings, should have a minimum of nine feet of clearance and be located in an area designed to discourage children from running into its path; the surface underneath such equipment should be soft sand or grass. The playground itself should be enclosed by a sufficiently high, nonclimbable fence or wall. In case of emergency, at least one exit (a secured one) should lead directly from the playground to the street.

5. *Roof playgrounds.* A roof playground limits the playing surfaces. There's no place for grass; sand must be kept in a sandbox and earth in window boxes. If there's no alternative, however, choose a surface that's safe for children. Asphalt pavement, possibly mixed with cork or sawdust, is more satisfactory than concrete. Enclose the entire roof playground with a sturdy, nonclimbable fence at least seven feet high. No climbing equipment should be placed within several feet of the fence. The playground must have a direct exit (with a child-proof lock) to a fire escape.

In warm weather, wading pools are a desirable addition to outdoor play, but care must be taken to keep them sanitary. Another feature of the playground that adds to the children's pleasure is a small hill or two, artificial or natural.

Building Safety

Preschool children have not yet developed the ability to differentiate between safety and danger. It is the responsibility of adults, therefore, to see to it that surroundings are safe. In most communities local building, fire, and safety laws must be adhered to, but not all of these laws take into consideration the special problems involved in the group care of young children. Here are some of the safety features especially applicable to a day care center:

1. *Fire protection.* Fire extinguishers should be placed in all parts of the building, but out of the reach of children. Classroom doors and building exits should open out. Every floor should have at least two widely separated outside exits. Fire escapes with child-proof fasteners at the entrances should be specially constructed for use by young children. A fire-alarm system is a most important safety measure, and fire drills should be a regular part of the center's program.

2. *Stairs and exits.* When possible, all rooms used by young children should be on the ground floor. (Some licensing regulations forbid the use of a floor higher than the second.) Ramps are safer for children than stairs. If stairs must be used, child-height bannisters should be provided, and all open stairwells completely closed off. All windows, galleries, terraces, and so on should have safety screens or bars of a type that children cannot climb on or through. All dangerous exits from the building should be equipped with child-proof fasteners. Doors habitually left unlocked should have child-proof knobs—too high for a child to reach.

3. *Electrical wiring.* Electrical outlets in all rooms used by children should have protective caps, and, if possible, should be placed above child height. If the building is old, electrical wiring in the walls as well as the outlets must be checked periodically to eliminate fire hazards.

4. *Heating.* The building should use central heating. The furnace or central burner should be completely enclosed in a room of fireproof construction and inspected regularly. Any exposed radiators should have a protective covering.

5. *Fans.* Portable fans, even if enclosed, should not be used near young children. When fans are necessary, they should be installed in the ceiling or high on the walls.

6. *Floor surfaces.* Because the children will sit on them, floors should be smooth and splinterproof. Highly polished, slippery floors, however, are dangerous for running, playing children and for the adults who have to move quickly to keep up with them. Rooms with different floor levels are also hazards. Rises should be made into ramps.

7. *Equipment.* All furniture, toys, and play equipment used by children must be kept free from splinters and protruding nails, and, if painted, be painted with lead-free paint. They should be checked frequently for signs of wear that could cause accidents.

8. *Elevator and building inspection.* If the children must use an elevator, it should be the safest type available. In addition to routine inspections of the elevator by building authorities, a company specializing in elevator maintenance should conduct regular checkups. Older buildings should also be examined periodically by construction engineers to make certain they are structurally sound enough for use by groups of active children.

Caution: Know your local building codes and fire regulations.

Sanitation

Health and safety can be jeopardized just as much by unsanitary conditions as by an unsound building. Young children are even more dependent upon good hygiene and sanitation than are adults. When children are brought together in groups, the risk of spreading infections increases. Lack of building sanitation is a major contributing factor. Local sanitation laws, like building safety codes, may or may not have been written with group care of young children in mind. Every day care center must pay special attention to the following:

1. *Water.* A safe supply of water for handwashing, drinking, cooking, and washing dishes is absolutely essential.

2. *Sewage disposal and drainage systems.* Because these can be dangerous sources of infection, they must be installed by experts and approved by sanitation authorities. Sanitary garbage disposal is very important. All garbage receptacles must be covered and should be emptied frequently.

3. *Food.* Staff members who handle food should, insofar as possible, do no other work in the building. The entire staff of the center should have regular physical examinations, but food handlers must have even more comprehensive examinations at more frequent intervals. Sanitary methods of food handling should be taught to all kitchen personnel, with constant supervision to be sure that these methods are followed. Dishes used by groups of children must be sterilized; the kitchen installations should make provisions for such sterilization, including a supply of hot water with a temperature of 180°F.[7] Chemical sterilization is acceptable. Either method depends on thorough rinsing to avoid soap or chemical residue on the dishes.

Safe storage of food is as important as building safety. This means refrigeration for perishable foods; dry, ventilated areas for cereals, grains, and vegetables; and tightly covered cans for dry foods bought in bulk. A regular insect-control program is essential for the food-storage kitchen areas.

4. *Cleaning.* The entire building must at all times be clean and sanitary. Children sit on floors, put things in their mouths, and touch food after they have played with toys. This means that classrooms and toys must be cleaned frequently. (A special staff should be assigned to cleaning duties only. Teachers cannot leave children alone while they attend to such tasks.) All floors, walls, and furniture in classrooms, the kitchen, and toilet rooms should be of easily washable material. Special attention should be given to cleaning toilet rooms and the kitchen because these are the areas from which infectious diseases can easily be spread.

5. *Screens.* Good ventilation, either with windows or air-conditioning, is necessary, particularly in the kitchen and toilet rooms. All windows, however, must be safely screened against flies and other insects.

6. *Disposal of supplies.* The use of disposable diapers and cleaning

---

[7] This temperature is too hot for faucets in children's washrooms.

cloths is recommended to prevent the spread of infection. Careful handling and removal, especially of diapers, is important to maintaining a safe and sanitary environment.

Caution: Comply with all local laws for fire, sanitation, and building safety; then add your own special precautions.

Comfort

Comfort is not a luxury for young children. It is an important contribution to their good health as well as to their sense of well-being. Some conditions are required by law; others depend on your knowledge of what makes young children comfortable.

1. *Ventilation and heat.* Sufficient fresh air is necessary for every room. If there are not enough windows, artificial ventilation should be supplied. Rooms used by children should be free from drafts or overheating. A temperature of 68° to 72°F at child height is comfortable. Carpeting a portion of the floor area has advantages in creating a warm environment. An uncarpeted section of the floor facilitates cleanup of wet activities such as water play and painting. Every playroom should have outside windows, preferably at child height, so that the children can look out.

2. *Illumination.* Good light is important both to safeguard the children's vision and to afford a sense of well-being. In almost all regions of the country, artificial light is needed to supplement natural illumination on dark days. A brightness of 25 to 35 footcandles is recommended. Windows should be fitted with adjustable shades or blinds to protect against glare and to darken the room for naptime.

3. *Soundproofing.* This is highly desirable in classrooms. Soundproofing reduces fatigue for both children and staff members and, especially in a multifunction building, makes it easier for the day care center to have good relations with its neighbors.

4. *Color.* Children respond to attractive colors. Classrooms should be painted in light (but not bright or garish) colors pleasing to children. Care should be taken that the paint is lead-free and does not produce glare.

Equipment
for the Day Care Center[8]

The equipment in the day care center is as important as the building itself, and this is especially true when the building is not an ideal one to begin with. Installations and furnishings may make up for a number of deficiencies.

Permanent Installations

Kitchen fixtures—stove, refrigerator, dishwasher, sinks—must be efficient, hygienic, and of the right type and size to serve a large number of children and adults.

Toilet and Handwashing Facilities

Child-size toilets and washbowls are needed in a sufficient number and in the right places. Mirrors placed at child height in the toilet room should be considered part of the basic installation; mirrors are an important means of teaching children to help themselves.

Furnishings for Adults

1. *For offices.* Furniture and office equipment to make it possible for the people working in these offices to do their jobs efficiently

---

[8] See Appendix A for a list of items.

2. *For staff rest rooms.* Comfortable furniture in a pleasant, although not necessarily luxurious, environment conducive to relaxation

3. *For meeting rooms.* Enough chairs, a table, and some attractive decoration

Equipment and Furnishings for Children

All equipment and furnishings in the children's playrooms should be selected in relation to the children's needs and the center's program. Educational materials (toys, arts and crafts supplies, etc.) are the teacher's tools. With them a teacher provides the children with educational and social experiences and physical exercise. Even when the center must watch its budget, economies should not be made in essential equipment for the children.

The same basic equipment is needed in all centers—no matter what auspices they are under or by what name they are called—if the children are to have a program that contributes to their all-around development, growth, and happiness. The following are criteria for the selection of furnishings and equipment for the playrooms of a day care center:

1. *Child-size furniture.* The type of furniture provided for the children plays a part in their physical development because it affects posture and fatigue. Chairs should be the right height for the children's feet to rest comfortably on the floor. Backs of chairs should give support. Tables should be high enough so that the children's knees do not bump the table, yet low enough for eating and working. Since children of the same age are not of equal height, at least two different heights of tables and chairs may be needed in each classroom. Open shelves at child height, with divisions of varying sizes, make toys and supplies easily accessible to the children and encourage them to put back materials in an orderly way.

2. *Safe and durable equipment.* Toys should be painted with nontoxic paints; have no splinters, sharp edges, or protruding nails; and always be in good repair. Equipment that breaks easily tends to discourage children from learning how to take care of it. Also, fragile equipment may cause accidents.

3. *Ample supplies.* When there is not enough equipment, children may be deprived of the chance to play together and thus learn social behavior. An inadequate supply means that some children will feel left out and others will become overly competitive. Children need to be occupied; if they do not have materials to keep them busy, they become restless and sometimes quarrelsome and destructive.

If the budget is limited, emphasize materials that help the children create and use their imaginations. Constructing something with a set of blocks keeps children occupied much longer and gives them a greater feeling of achievement than playing with a single expensive mechanical toy or even an expensive table game. Children prefer toys like blocks, clay, paints, crayons, small cubes, small figures of people and animals, and dolls and housekeeping equipment in a housekeeping corner of the room.

Since the center's program is planned for a group of children, not just for the individual child, it is important to choose equipment that lends itself to the stimulation of cooperative play. For example, if there is a choice between buying one or two tricycles, which only one child can ride at a time, and a jungle gym that many children can climb together, choose the jungle gym. For the same reasons, a wagon is preferable to a swing. Only one child at a time can use a swing, but a wagon gives one child a chance to pull and one more a chance to ride.

The Staff of the Day Care Center

Although a good building and good equipment are important, even more important to the day care center is its staff. They are the people who safeguard the children, plan and carry out the program, handle day-to-day problems and emergencies, and make the group experience a good or poor one for the children.

A day care center is one place where quality does not make up for insufficient quantity. Neither, however, does quantity replace quality. The center needs the best qualified people it can find, and it needs them in sufficient numbers so that the program described in this guide can be carried out.

The size of the staff depends on the number of children, on the special features of the center's program, and, to some extent, on the physical premises. Although the size of the staff may vary, its composition does not. Each of the following has a unique contribution to make to the day care program: director; teachers; kitchen and maintenance staff; office staff; bus drivers (if transportation is provided); and medical, mental health, and social service personnel on staff or as consultants.

In a small center the director may be able to fill a second job, depending on his or her professional background. If, for example, it is early childhood education, he or she can supervise the teaching staff; if it is social work, he or she may function as the social worker.

Whether the director can do two jobs depends upon the size of the center's population, the special needs of the children and their families, and the center's program. Under no circumstances can the director be expected to carry a regular teaching assignment with a group of children.

The administrative responsibilities are time-consuming, frequently of an urgent nature, and not compatible with providing the day-long relationship that children need with their teacher.

If the center is a large one, or if the director is a social worker, nurse, or other non-early-childhood educator, an educational supervisor for the teaching staff is necessary. If the director is an educator, however, a social worker sufficiently qualified and experienced to work without professional supervision should be part of the staff, unless the center is part of a multifunction agency that employs many social workers and has supervision available.

Size of the Teaching Staff

Teaching staff requirements must be considered in relation to the hours the center is open, how may children attend, and the special needs of these children. Other important factors in determining the size of the teaching staff are the number of children present at any given time during the day and how they are grouped.

For example, the center that really serves a neighborhood has children coming to it for many different reasons and with many different individual needs. Some children may be best served by attending only a few hours a day; others may benefit from attending for the major part of the day, and children of working parents may require care for long, full days.

If the majority of children come to the center for a major part of the day, it may be necessary to provide auxiliary staff for extended hours. If, however, a center has many half-day children, it may be better to establish separate groups for them. A large exodus at noon may upset the equilibrium of the children who stay longer. It may also change the nature of the relationships established among the children, since shared experiences are such an important factor in their friendships. (It is not a good idea to have children who come only in the afternoon join a group that is present for most of the day. The latter need a nap, and for the afternoon-session child, a nap is not usually the best introduction to the joys of group play.) But no matter how children are grouped, plans for the size of the teaching staff must take into account the necessity of responsible physical care and supervision as well as continuity in relationships. The following are factors to be considered:

1. Teachers (not bus drivers, cooks, or maintenance workers)

must be on duty from the moment the first child arrives at the center until the last child leaves.

2. Every group of preschool children needs two regularly assigned teachers.

3. It is highly desirable that all children be greeted individually when they arrive and be bade good-by at the end of the day by one of their group teachers. This is important not only for the child, but also for maintaining daily contact with parents.

4. Teachers cannot be expected to work more than seven or eight hours a day, and it is desirable that they not spend more than six hours working directly with children. Staggering teachers'/caregivers' working hours is necessary if the center is open for more than eight hours.

5. If only a few children from all groups come very early or stay very late, and the center's day is a long one, some children may have to be cared for by a teacher/caregiver other than their own at the beginning or end of the day. This is necessary if all of the teaching staff is to be present during the major part of the day.

6. When the working hours of the staff are staggered, it is important to rotate the schedules so that all of the children sometimes see their own teacher at the beginning or end of the day.

7. When many children arrive at the center very early and stay very late, additional teachers are needed. It is not a good idea to schedule these additional staff members as part-timers who come in at the end of the day to "baby-sit." At the end of the day, the children need someone who knows what they have been doing and how they have been feeling all day long, and who can give this information to their parents and get necessary information from them.

8. Additional staff members should be scheduled in such a way that there is overlapping, so the teachers can all work together for some hours each day and the children can know them as a team of teachers. The teachers should have the opportunity to exchange

knowledge about the children and to have a common program philosophy and a common method of dealing with children.

9. If it is necessary for the children to be greeted in the morning or turned over to their parents in the afternoon by a teacher other than the one who guides them for much of the day, it is imperative that whoever sees the parent knows what this child is usually like and what kind of day the child has had, and is prepared to understand and report anything the parents say to the child's regular teacher.

10. In planning for staff, it must be emphasized that children can never be left alone and that no teacher should be left with more than two children unless there is another adult within easy calling distance and available should an emergency occur.

Size of the Office, Kitchen, Maintenance, and Transportation Staff

The size and makeup of the secretarial and bookkeeping staff depends upon the size of the professional staff and the number and kinds of records kept. It is important to remember that teachers, as well as social workers, directors, and health personnel, keep records on the children's progress, and that these records eventually must be keyboarded into the permanent file for each child.

The kitchen and maintenance staff is determined by the size and type of the building, the kind of food served, and the number of times a day food is provided. In a multifunction building, heavy cleaning and building maintenance may be provided by the building administration, but the center still needs its own staff for the daily cleaning of children's playrooms, equipment, and toilets. In a building used exclusively for day care, a maintenance person may also act as guard if necessary. If a center provides transportation, the number of bus drivers depends on the number of children to be transported. In deciding whether to provide transportation, it is important to note that a transportation system more often than not eliminates the valuable daily contact between teachers and parents.

Job Definitions and Staff Qualifications

The staff of a day care center should have the special knowledge and special personal qualifications necessary for planning and carrying out the center's program. Good will and love for children are most important, but they are not a substitute for the knowledge needed to care for and safeguard groups of young children and stimulate their healthy development. Each center has to work out its own job definitions and criteria for staff selection, based on the complexity of its program, community needs, and local regulations. Once the work of the various staff members has been defined, it is easier to know what qualifications to look for. Finding them may not be easy. But if a given job can be done only by a person with certain training, and there is no such person in the community, it may be necessary to bring in someone from another area. It may also be necessary for the community to set up local training facilities so that trained personnel will be available. Local recruitment and training are especially important if the community to be served has specific language and/or cultural characteristics.

The Director

Directing a day care center is quite different from running a household, even though young children and their families are involved. It is a job that has many facets. The duties are varied, requiring not only contacts with a great variety of people, but also a knowledge of many types of work and different professional skills. It has been said that anyone who can run a really good day care center and give the right emphasis to each different aspect of the job could be president of the United States!

The director's ability to organize and administer all the different aspects of the program determines how effectively the staff members carry out their jobs and how much the children ultimately benefit from the program.

Responsibilities

The director must:

Be responsible to the governing body of the center. This responsibility is threefold: to conduct the program of the day care center in accordance with policies established by the governing body; to inform the governing body of the needs of the children, the staff, and the parents in order to establish new policies and revise old ones; and to aid the governing body in formulating policy and planning for the future.

Employ and supervise staff. The director makes recommendations to the governing body on the number and kind of staff members needed. The director is solely responsible, however, for interviewing, employing, and dismissing staff members within the personnel policies established by the governing body. The director establishes the work schedules, being mindful of the children's needs, the importance of consistency in caregiving, and the need for a continuously safe and healthy environment. In a day care center, there are many people with different jobs and skills (teachers, cooks, bus drivers, maintenance workers, and consultants) who work together. How well they perform depends on the ability of the director to weld them into a team. It is up to the director to establish procedures for the various jobs, see that they are followed, and provide the proper tools and equipment. Although supervision for the professional aspects of a given staff member's work may come not from the director but rather from a person with that professional skill, the director nevertheless sees that each staff member functions within the established goals, policies, and procedures of the center. The director establishes an atmosphere of mutual respect and harmony that enables all staff members to contribute their best. To do this, the director must meet frequently with the staff, individually and in groups, to discuss their plans and problems, provide opportunities for them to exchange information, and encourage them to make program suggestions and find ways to use their ideas.

Organize all aspects of the program. Many activities take place in a day care center at the same time—the continuing developmental play and education of the children, meal service, health care, contacts with parents, and so on. The director must understand the principles underlying all aspects of the program. The director may not take an active part in all of them, but should know each role well enough to take the practical steps necessary to keep the program operating effectively. It is the director who, with overall knowledge, plans the time schedules so that teachers are on duty when the children arrive, the building is cleaned without disturbing the children, food is ready at the proper time and the children are ready for it, and the many details of operation run smoothly. Delegation of specific jobs to specific staff members is also an important aspect of the director's work to be sure that everyone can function responsibly.

Purchase all equipment and supplies. The director makes purchases of equipment and supplies, with both the children's needs and budget limitations in mind, keeps an up-to-date inventory of equipment and supplies, and is familiar with the general condition of the building. It is the director's responsibility to keep expenditures within the budget and to anticipate the center's requirements so that the governing body can provide necessary funds. The director may authorize other staff members to make specific purchases or spend a given amount of money for certain supplies over a period of time. For example, teachers may each receive an allotment for special supplies for a certain project or for a trip. The director, however, exercises final control over how this money is spent.

Establish and maintain reports and records. The efficient operation of any organization requires that certain records and reports be maintained, and a day care center is no exception. The director must see to it that financial accounts, inventories, personnel files, and such are always up to date and, if possible, computerized for ready access. In addition, the center needs full and up-to-date information on each child and the child's family, health status, attendance patterns, and progress. It is the director's responsibility to have this information compiled regularly and kept confidential.

Facilitate close relationships between the parents and the staff. The director sets the tone for a cooperative relationship with parents. The director makes parents feel welcome and keeps them informed about the center, its activities, and its plans, and encourages staff-parent contacts by providing a comfortable meeting place and arranging staff time for such meetings. The director also helps staff members plan ways to strengthen their relationships with parents, and lets parents know that they matter by respecting their opinions, their suggestions, and their complaints.

Interpret the program of the center to the community. The director must know how to describe the center's program so that other community agencies and visitors to the center understand the part the center plays in the life of the children and the community. The director should be able to give some time to serving on community planning committees and to establishing relationships with other agencies and services in the community that may be helpful to the children or their families.

Interpret the community to the staff. The director has to keep informed about community services, agencies, and changes (new housing projects, local economic developments, etc.) that can affect the lives of the children and the future of the day care center, and bring this information to the staff, and, when appropriate, to the governing body.

Promote staff development. All professional people make their greatest contribution when they have opportunities for continuing growth on the job. Staff meetings, supervisory help, training programs, attendance at conferences, leaves of absence for study, access to new professional literature, and access to outside consultants through seminars are all ways to stimulate staff growth and development. The director must plan for all of these, and also make sure that all new staff members are properly oriented.

Professional Qualifications

The director of a day care center should be a graduate of an accredited school and qualified in early childhood education, child development, social work, or a related field. It cannot be stressed too strongly that a center director should also have several years of experience in the profession after training, since the director's job involves not only ultimate responsibility for the children's safety and development, but also the judicious handling of many different people and activities. For this complicated job, the director needs special personal and professional qualifications. As a person, the director should be mature, be able to instill confidence and respect in other people, use authority constructively, have good judgment, and not be afraid to make decisions and take responsibility for them. The director must be able to plan his or her own work and that of the staff, to delegate responsibility, and to handle many problems at a time without becoming confused or upset. A director should have a deep respect for the worth of each individual and show this respect to parents, staff, and children. Finally, a director must understand children and childhood, be firmly convinced that the care and development of young children are of the utmost importance, and find pleasure and satisfaction in the work.

The Educational Supervisor

If the director is not qualified in the field of early childhood education, or if the center is a very large one, an educational supervisor is needed to plan and direct the children's program, to supervise the teachers in their work, and to plan and carry out staff development activities for the teachers.

The educational supervisor must be a graduate of an accredited school of early childhood education and must have had several years' experience teaching young children. The supervisor must know how to plan and direct the activities of a group of teachers; be capable of evaluating their performance; and give the kind of help that will enable them to increase their skills—all in the context of understanding the overall goals of the center, the role of the teachers, and the implications in the daily activities of the children. The supervisor must be familiar with and have an understanding of the community: its cultural aspects, its resources, its institutions, and its service agencies.

The educational supervisor should have maturity, objectivity, and the ability to relate to many different kinds of people.

The Teacher

Not everyone can be a teacher of young children. A teacher must have more than just a love for children. A teacher should be firmly convinced that the first years of a child's life are important, and should have the patience to help a child through the trial and error of these years. A teacher has to understand teaching in its broadest sense—as an education for life—and to be aware that all the roots of more formal learning stem from these early years. A teacher has to be more than merely kind and gentle to children, and do more than help them learn to pass tests. A teacher must be able to help each child realize his or her individual potential.

A teacher of young children should have:

A warm, sympathetic, friendly personality. Teachers must really enjoy being with children, show it in action, and let children feel they can look to them for protection, help, and sympathy.

Self-confidence. Teachers must be able to give children the feeling that they know what they are doing and for what reasons. The teachers' self-confidence helps the children feel secure with them.

Dependability and stability. Not only should teachers understand their individual responsibility for safeguarding, protecting, and teaching children; they must also be able to use good judgment in emergencies and in their reactions to any unusual behavior of children or colleagues.

Ability to accept supervision. Teachers must be able to learn new concepts and know how and when to use what they have learned. They must be capable of accepting criticism without defensiveness and of continuing to experiment and try out new ideas without fear of failure.

Good health. Teachers must be in good physical and mental health. Keeping up physically with active preschoolers requires vigorous activity. And sharing the care of a child with the parents requires that teachers know their role in the child's life and realize that they cannot fulfill their own emotional needs by becoming a rival of the parents for the child's affections.

Responsibilities

To do the job well, a teacher must be able to:

- Direct the activities of an assistant teacher so that the two teachers work as a team

- Plan and carry out the daily activities of the children

- Prepare and arrange all necessary educational materials

- Keep the classroom in order and equipment in good condition

- Attend staff meetings; share information and planning with all members of the center's staff

- Attend parent meetings

- Share information about the child with the parents and plan with them to meet the child's needs

Professional Qualifications

A teacher of preschool children should be a graduate of an accredited school of early childhood education or child development and have some teaching experience.

The Assistant Teacher

To the young child, the assistant teacher is as important as the head teacher. The individual personality characteristics and needs of the children may incline them to relate more closely to a particular teacher without regard to status or professional background, and it is important for the children's development that they be able to do so. Both the teacher and the assistant teacher must represent authority, love, and protection. At times, the assistant teacher will be required to take temporary responsibility for the group; unless the children regard the assistant as "teacher," with all that the word implies, she or he will be unable to do so successfully. Therefore, the assistant teacher should have the same personal qualifications as the head teacher.

Responsibilities

The duties of the assistant teacher vary only slightly from those of the head teacher. The assistant teacher's job is to:

- Assist the teacher throughout the day in the care and education of the children

- Take responsibility for the group for short periods of time, as required

- Accept the philosophy and programming techniques of the head teacher and learn to work as part of a team

- Assist in the care of classroom and supplies

- Attend staff meetings

- Attend parent meetings

- Share with the teacher information gained from casual contacts with parents

- Be informed about the status of each child and family so that even casual contacts with parents reflect a consistent approach on the part of the day care center

Professional Qualifications

The assistant teacher may be recruited from any of several different backgrounds. The ideal situation is for the center to attract new graduates of early childhood education programs who will work for one or two years as assistant teachers to gain the experience necessary to carry overall responsibility for a group. This provides a line of succession for head teacher vacancies. Assistant teachers may also be persons qualified in related fields who want some experience before going on to further study. In parent-cooperative centers, the assistant teacher may be the parent of one of the children. If a center is set up for training or is affiliated with an educational institution, the assistant teacher may be a student.

Teachers' Aides and Volunteers

Although there is no substitute for a trained teacher, there is room on the day care center's staff for people without professional skills. In the highly labor intensive field of day care it is especially important that centers recognize aides and volunteers as valuable resources and offer them training and supervised classroom experience as a way of meeting the professional labor shortage. Sometimes these aides can be volunteers, sometimes paid assistants to teachers.

How untrained staff members are used depends very much on whether the center is prepared to give in-service training as well as supervision. It also depends on the needs of the children served by the center. For example, young children away from their parents for most of the day are especially dependent on the adults in the center for stability, continuity, and skillful, knowledgeable response to their needs.

Under certain circumstances, older teenagers are capable of learning some basic principles of handling young children and the routines associated with groups of children, and can perform well as paid assistants. They can function as third "teachers" for a group that spends many hours at the center. For a group that spends only a few hours a day at the center, they may be second "teachers." This work experience is constructive and may encourage them to go on with their studies and become qualified teachers.

Likewise, with the growth of intergenerational programs, senior citizens may be valuable as paid or volunteer auxiliary personnel.

It must be stressed, however, that untrained staff members should not be engaged unless there is an established, ongoing plan for in-service training and supervision. This means there must be a series of discussions and workshops—not just a single orientation session—to acquaint the untrained staff with program content and to teach them the techniques of handling young children in groups. It means, also, that these staff members must generally work side by side with a qualified teacher who is prepared to offer supervision.

Volunteers cannot take the place of paid staff unless the volunteer is that rarity who is professionally educated and experienced and can volunteer on a full-time basis. In most cases volunteers are available only for specified times. They have much to contribute, but should not be considered as substitutes for the permanent, full-time, paid teacher. Young children cannot respond positively to a succession of adults caring for them in rotation. Even when volunteers act as assistants to the regular teacher, not too many volunteers should be present at the same time. Volunteers should come regularly enough for the children to get to know them and to look forward to their presence as individual, friendly, helpful adults.

Volunteers and aides can offer many enriching services to the day care center. They can:

- Assist the teacher with activities and routines

- Give special attention and help to a child who needs it

- Use their special talents in art or music to enrich the children's experiences

- Accompany the children and their teacher on excursions into the community

After they are accustomed to the children's and the center's routines, volunteers and aides can supervise the children's naptime while the teachers attend a staff meeting. They can also render invaluable assistance as replacements on days when a regular teacher is absent.

Jobs that do not involve working with the children at the center can also be done by volunteers, who can:

- Serve as board members

- Organize and conduct fund-raising projects for the center

- Assist in the office by answering telephones, typing, and acting as receptionists

- Help parents with some of their group activities

- Make doll clothes, mend toys and books, paint furniture, construct new equipment for the children, and make other needed improvements in the facility

- Provide child care for parents who otherwise could not come to a meeting at the center

- Escort children to and from the center

No matter what professional or personal skills volunteers and aides bring to the center, they need orientation in the work of the day care program and supervision for ongoing participation. In-service training programs especially for volunteers and aides are a most effective means of enabling them to make their greatest contributions and of ensuring their continuing interest and satisfaction in the work.

Kitchen, Office, Transportation, and Maintenance Staff

In hiring the kitchen, office, transportation, and maintenance staff, care should be taken to select people who like children and have the patience to do their work among them. All the adults in the day care center are important to the children. The relationships they have with the cooks, office personnel, maintenance staff, and bus drivers play a significant part in their education.

Auxiliary Personnel

The Physician Consultant

The center's consulting physician should preferably be a pediatrician and, if possible, have some training or background in public health, because of the hazards to health inherent in bringing young children together in groups.

The physician should help the staff to plan and organize the center's health program and supervise all its aspects, and be available to staff members and parents for consultation on health problems and for emergencies. The physician may also give such direct services as are indicated by the local situation. When a nurse is employed, the doctor is responsible for planning and supervising the nurse's activities.

If a private physician with these qualifications is not available, the center should try to obtain the services of a qualified doctor on a consultancy basis from the nearest public health or hospital facility.

The Part-Time or Consultant Nurse

The nurse employed by a day care center should have public health training. In most day care centers nursing services are needed only part time, and these services may be obtained directly or through an arrangement with a community public health agency.

The nurse assists the doctor and the staff in establishing the health plan for the center and helps teachers to understand the health needs of children, providing practical training for daily inspection and ongoing observation and establishing and supervising procedures for maintaining the children's health records. The nurse should be available to parents both for individual conferences and for group meetings.

Even a very small center can usually obtain the services of a nurse on an hourly basis. If this is impossible, the responsibilities usually assigned to the nurse must be divided among the doctor, the director, the teachers, and the social worker.

The Social Worker or Social Work Consultant

The social worker or social work consultant in a day care center should have a degree, preferably from an accredited school of social work, plus some experience in working with young children and parents. Maturity is of the utmost importance, and the social worker should be a person sufficiently experienced to work without supervision, since in most cases she or he will be the only person on the day care center staff with that particular professional background. The social worker should have many of the same personal characteristics as the teachers and the director— empathy with parents and children, warmth, ability to work as a member of a team, respect for the individual worth of each person, good judgment, and stability in making day-to-day and emergency decisions.

A professional social worker brings to the day care center the knowledge and skills for helping parents and children with problems that affect their relationship, with problems in their environment, and with problems affecting the rearing and development of children. When necessary, the social worker can help parents make use of community services. As a member of the staff team, the social worker can contribute an understanding of family relationships, the dynamics of human behavior, and the possible effects of separation—even for short periods of time—on both children and parents. The social worker can also participate in community planning for child welfare services and provide training and consultation on how to recognize possible child abuse or neglect and how to report evidence of abuse or neglect.

The social worker's contacts with parents do not take the place of those between the teacher and the parents, nor of the contacts that parents have from time to time with the health staff or with the director. The social worker is a member of the staff team with full knowledge and appreciation of each staff member's contribution. Adding a social work component enhances the center's program by providing additional support services when appropriate; for example, to parents of children with special needs.

It would be unrealistic to say that a day care center cannot be run without a social worker. If the center is too small to warrant having its own full-time social worker, it is possible, in most communities, to arrange for part-time services from a child welfare, family service, or mental health agency on a consultancy basis.

Mental Health Personnel

Mental health consultation services may be obtained directly by the day care center from child psychiatrists, psychologists, or clinical social workers on a fee basis, or through a community mental health agency. If these arrangements are not possible, it is important that the center establish contact with whatever mental health diagnostic and treatment resources exist in the community so that referrals can be made when necessary.

What Is the Day Care Center Program?

The program of the day care center is much more than a schedule of daily activities. It is the means by which we bring all the center's resources to the children to help them develop as individuals and as members of the group, the family, and the community. The program is the expression of the day care concept. It is the result of combining knowledge about the child and the family with the various professional skills to make best use of that knowledge.

Today we recognize the interdependence of the child's physical, emotional, intellectual, and social growth and the importance of the child's interrelationships with the family and the center. That is why the program must comprise many different aspects—play, health, education, welfare, physical care, and the relationship with parents. Each is equally important, and none can be left out. Nor can any of them be given to the child separately, like doses of medicine. Every part of the program must be incorporated in some way into all of the child's activities at the center.

The program, then, represents the hopes and aspirations of the staff members for the child's best development. In essence, it is the sum total of their skills and knowledge; it is a planned environment for the children, and it is also the relationship between the parents and the staff.

Each staff member offers his or her specialized skills and draws on those of other staff members. The center's activities, policies, rules and regulations, and schedules are planned jointly by staff members representing each aspect of the program.

A day care center's program is much like a recipe. When certain ingredients are combined, the result is a product different from any of its components. In cooking, whether the finished dish is what you expected or wanted depends on your using all the necessary ingredients in the right proportions. Varying the proportions or omitting one or more of the ingredients may produce an entirely different dish. So it is with a day care center program. Not only is it necessary to combine the ingredients well, but it is also important to be sure that all the ingredients are included. Otherwise, the program will not turn out as expected.

Daily Schedules

Young children develop best with a regular (but not rigid) schedule. They feel most secure with the familiar, and want to find the same things in the same place every day. They like routines and enjoy knowing what comes next. Because their growth requires that physical needs be attended to at certain intervals, activities are planned with these needs in mind. Exciting events like the celebration of holidays, birthdays, and trips into the community are kept simple and are fitted into the daily routine. Even the maintenance work of the center is planned around the children's daily time schedule so that it will not interfere with their regular activities. Only in the rarest emergencies is there any deviation from the time schedule, and in a well-run day care center emergencies are rare.

Time schedules change with the seasons to allow for outdoor play according to the weather. The schedules also vary for different age groups within the same center. Younger children need more rest or sleep and more frequent toileting. They need more time for routines because they are slower and less independent, and less time for some activities because they have shorter interest spans than older children.

Within the framework of a well-balanced daily time schedule, however, great flexibility is possible. The skillful teacher who knows the children well recognizes restlessness with one activity and substitutes another. When the teacher notices a child getting sleepy in mid-morning, it is time to give him or her a chance to sleep. When the children are deeply absorbed in a learning experience, the teacher lets them continue with it instead of changing to the activity the schedule calls for, unless it is mealtime or naptime. Flexibility enables the day care program to meet the children's needs, but it is the teacher's skill that keeps flexibility from turning into chaos.

Here are some of the program activities that should take place at the center every day:

- Contacts between parents and staff members

- Health supervision

- Physical care and protection of the child

- Supervised play—indoors and out

- Vigorous physical activity

- Creative arts—reading, crafts, drawing, painting, music, dance, and dramatic play

- Social relationships

- Routines—washing, eating, toileting, and sleeping or resting

The daily schedule should be planned so that there is a good balance between quiet and active experiences. Time should also be allowed for food at required intervals.

Time schedules vary at different centers because schedules depend upon how many hours the children spend at the center and their special requirements. Every time schedule must be planned with the 24-hour needs of the children in mind. It should take into consideration the home situation as well as the center activities.

This guide cannot fix the exact sequence of activities or detail the procedures in each day care center program, but it does give some principles and objectives of a good program. It cannot be stated too strongly that no one aspect of the program is more important than another; certain parts, however, may be emphasized differently, depending upon the special needs of the children and their families.

Educational Aspects

Education begins with birth and continues to the end of life. It is concerned with learning attitudes as well as skills and facts. Young children learn something every minute of their waking hours. They learn from contacts with people and things; from new experiences and the repetition of previous experiences; from moments of happiness, fear, anger, or desolation; and from language and music and all the other sounds that surround them.

The day care center plays a large part in this learning. It offers the child specific, planned learning situations, and it also offers many casual ones. But planned or not, good or bad, the child learns something from each experience. This is why center staff must be well aware of what is being taught.

Because the child's education goes on all day, it is a mistake to designate one part of the daily activities as the "educational program."

Professionally educated and trained staff members know how a young child learns. They set the stage so that the right kind of learning takes place from the moment the children enter the center until they leave. This learning includes capitalizing on spontaneous situations. Young children learn a good deal from observation and from feeling. The staff sees to it that what goes on around the children is as helpful to their developing perceptions and concepts as are the situations in which they participate directly. How the child is greeted in the morning, how the teacher talks to the parents, how the director speaks to the teacher, how the teacher speaks to the maintenance staff—all contribute to the children's view of patterns of behavior in the world around them. These are the reasons why everyone working at the center must understand the true meaning of education for the children and share the same goals for them. Only when this is true can we say that the children's developmental needs are being met, that the interrelationship of the physical, emotional, intellectual, and social aspects of their growth is recognized and nourished.

The Teacher's Role

The teacher is the individual through whom all the benefits of the center's program reach the child. The teacher is responsible for the care and guidance of the group and for each child within the group. The teacher is an educator in the broadest sense because she or he is concerned with all aspects of the child's growth and development, holding the key to the success or failure of all the available program services—health, education, care, protection, social work, and psychological and psychiatric services.

The teacher's skill provides the setting as well as the climate of friendliness, guidance, and interest necessary to promote developmental opportunities. The following are some of the things a teacher does to make the day care center group a happy, satisfying, learning place for the child:

- Create a classroom atmosphere in which the children can grow from within according to their own needs and capacities at each stage of growth

- Support the children in the face of conflicts, failures, obstacles, and disappointments, and help them achieve new skills that enable them to cope better and better with similar situations

- Use special skill to set limits necessary for the age of the children and adapt those limits to their strides in growth

- Talk to the children in language they can understand and respond to them in both words and actions

- Understand that young children's behavior is their way of telling the teacher how they feel, and watch their behavior closely for clues on how to help and guide them

- Use nonpunitive methods of dealing with out-of-bounds behavior, always aware that the goal is to develop self-discipline, not submission

- Provide a variety of materials selected with the developmental characteristics of the young child in mind

- Arrange toys and materials and make space available for their use so that the children can benefit from them

- Give the children free choice in selection of equipment, observe their use of it, stand ready to help them, and guide them toward new ways of using the equipment for richer achievements

- Make the classroom a place where the child finds order but not regimentation, freedom but not license

- Help the children gain satisfaction through growing competence in their own work rather than through competitive activity

- Help the children have satisfying experiences in their relationships with other children

- Know how to make routines as well as play activities good learning experiences

- Protect the children from danger

- Be aware of the children's physical condition at all times

- Understand the importance of your role as an adult in the life of the child and use this role to reinforce the children's sense of security and belonging

- Know the children's families and be familiar with their home situations

- Be prepared to seek consultation and make referrals when there are indications of child abuse or neglect

All this means that the teacher must be constantly aware of all of the children's needs and abilities in order to guide them well. Conversely, the children must know their teacher well if they are to respond to the teacher's guidance. Young children need a warm, close relationship with one or two familiar adults, and the younger they are the more this is true. They feel lost until that relationship is established.

Each group must have its own teacher and assistant teacher who live with the children all the time they are in the center. It can be very disturbing for a child to have a different teacher every few hours or on alternate days of the week. Such a staffing plan also defeats the educational goals. When several teachers are involved with a group on a rotating schedule, there is bound to be a lack of consistency in handling routines and setting limits. The all-important knowledge that the teacher gains from watching the child is lost if the teacher is not there when the child has a frustrating experience or advances to a new achievement. The old saying that what is everybody's business is nobody's business certainly applies here. When there is a rotation of teachers through a young child's day or week, no one of them really knows how the child is developing.

Play Activities

For the preschool child, play is a way of learning and has the same meaning as does work or study for the adult. It is and should be the child's main business in life.

Through play, the child develops mentally, emotionally, physically, and socially, all at the same time. What children learn through play they learn positively because it is based on experience that is built into their muscles and feelings. Play corresponds to the child's urge to stretch the body and mind, to test new things, to make decisions, and to find friends. When properly guided and supervised, play can provide preschool children with most of the learning experiences appropriate to their age.

The child's activities in the day care center, therefore, should be centered on a play program interspersed with routines necessary for physical well-being. When guided by skilled teachers, play can contain the child's first lessons in science, language, the arts, mathematics, and social studies. Play opens the child's mind and sets a firm foundation for later formal studies. The following are a few examples of what the child learns from play:

When children build with blocks, they

- Have the satisfaction of making something

- Use their imaginations to create

- Learn about sizes and shapes, weights and balances, height and depth, smoothness and roughness

- Develop manual control

- Get much-needed muscular exercise

- Learn the joy of doing something with another child and of working as a member of a team

- Develop a sense of order—when they put the blocks away, they learn how to fit the blocks together so that they go on the shelf in neat piles, and by putting the blocks on the shelf, they contribute to the orderly life of the classroom

- Master mathematical concepts.

When children paint a picture, they

- Learn to use their imaginations and transfer their ideas to paper

- Learn about colors and how they can mix and use them

- Learn about the physical properties of paint

- Get emotional satisfaction from being able to express themselves freely

- Develop fine-muscle coordination in handling the brush

When children play in the doll corner, they

- Explore their ideas of what parents and children are like and how they behave

- Understand what it feels like to pretend to be someone other than themselves

- Learn to share and cooperate with other children

When children make a gift to take home, they

- Learn to do things for others

- Learn how to use materials like scissors, paste, and paper

- Learn how to make decisions about what gift to make and how to make it

- Learn about shapes, sizes, colors, textures, and qualities of materials

When children climb on the jungle gym, they

- Learn how to use their bodies effectively

- Realize the limitations of their bodies

- Become aware of safety and caution

- Learn to share equipment with others

- Understand they must wait their turn when necessary

- Experience joy in achieving the skill of climbing

- Discover the relaxation to be found in bodily movement

Merely putting children and play materials together, however, does not automatically produce either a happy situation for the children or one in which good learning takes place. On the contrary, group play by young children, unless it is constructively guided, may be a destructive experience. The children may break or throw toys instead of playing or creating with them; they may use physical force ᵗo get what they want rather than learning to take turns and to respect the rights of others; and those on the losing end of battles with their playmates may learn to fear contact with other children. The teacher makes the difference in the meaning play activities can have for a group of children.

When parents and visitors observe a child during a period of supervised play, it is sometimes difficult for them to believe that the play is an educational experience, and that the teacher is actually teaching. They may think that things are happening without plan, on the spur of the moment, but it is not so. The teacher understands that offering the children a free choice of play activity is the best way to ensure that what they choose to do will interest them. But the teacher also knows how to stimulate the children's interest in trying out new materials and activities. Social experiences that come about naturally during play activities are an important part of the child's learning. The teacher knows how to foster the kind of play that will provide satisfying social experiences.

The teacher has a plan for the gradual introduction of new materials and experiences calculated to widen the child's horizons and to provide opportunities for growth in social relationships. Furthermore, the teacher has certain goals and objectives for the children's growth as individuals, and uses both planned and spontaneous opportunities to help them take the next steps on their way.

We cannot here describe in detail just how the teacher wields the magic that turns a number of individual preschoolers into a group of children involved in purposeful and meaningful activity. We do wish to stress, however, that in order to do the job, the teacher needs the following:

- Appropriate space

- Appropriate equipment and materials in adequate supply

- Small groups of children (size of group varies with age)

- Groups consisting of children of the same age (a wide age range requires a more skillful staff and more space)

- Permanent, full-time assignment of two teachers to a group (at least one fully qualified teacher and an assistant)

When these conditions prevail, a day care center can offer pre-school children something that almost no home can give them—an environment planned to make their play as meaningful and as satisfying as possible.

Routines

The day care center offers an especially fine opportunity to give young children some basic training in good habits. The matter-of-fact attitude of the teacher makes essential routines a normal, uncomplicated part of everyday living. Routines such as eating, sleeping, washing, toileting, putting on their hats and coats, combing their hair, cleaning up the classroom, and helping to set the table and serve the meal give the children an opportunity not only to develop their skills in handling these procedures and to learn how to take care of themselves, but also to feel that they are contributing to the daily living of the group. Because they do all this as members of a group, they can learn much by observation and by imitation. Also, they can often be freed from the tensions that surround some of these activities at home.

Children want to be like other children, and they want to please the teacher. The preschool age is the prime time for learning good habits and good attitudes toward the routines of living. Thus, the teacher supervises routine activities as carefully and thoughtfully as play activities, and sees attention to routine not as a menial task but as an excellent opportunity to educate children in the skills, attitudes, and habits they need for better living.

Meals and Snacks

At a day care center, eating, whether it be a snack or a hot meal, is a pleasant social affair. Teachers sit down to eat with the children. Good manners are suggested by example and by quietly offered help with difficult foods, never by edict. The teacher wants the children to learn to eat a wide variety of foods with enjoyment and to have only pleasant associations with mealtimes. The teacher knows which foods an individual child may dislike and sees to it that helpings of these foods are small enough to encourage him or her to try them. The teacher does not force children to eat or show anxiety when they do not, knowing they will not starve if they miss a few meals while they discover that no one will force food on them. While preserving a fair system of rotation for helping so that each child has a turn, the teacher arranges for the poor eaters to have many chances to help set the table and serve the meal to their friends, because this often encourages them to approach the food with more anticipation.

Toilet and Handwashing Routines

The teacher sets the tone for toilet procedures just as for all activities of the day, and always accompanies new or very young children because they need help. The teacher sets up a schedule for taking the youngest ones, usually a few at a time, to the toilet to remind them of their needs, and makes sure that all the children learn good habits. As they grow older, the children should be free to go to the toilet alone, assuming that toilet rooms are adjacent to the classroom; otherwise, the teacher should accompany them. The teacher must be sure they have all equipment necessary for carrying out the routines they have been taught, and must always be available to the children who have special needs.

Sleeping or Resting

Whether the children require a nap on cots or only a short rest on mats to break the fatigue of a morning or afternoon session, the teacher makes resting time a normal and pleasant part of the day. A quiet manner and voice set the atmosphere. If the rest period is to be a nap, darkening the room helps the children fall asleep. Those who are restless and cannot sleep are quietly occupied while resting. The teacher does not force children to sleep, but does expect them to respect the sleep needs of the other children.

In all of these routines, it is the teacher who guides the children, suggests the correct way, helps them to help themselves, and praises them when they do something well. The teacher knows the abilities of each of the children and is careful not to discourage or shame them by demanding more than they can do.

Health, Hygiene, and Safety Issues

Health Aspects

Good health is fundamental to the all-round development of young children. Thus, health protection is a fundamental part of the day care center's program. This is provided for by the structure of the premises; safety measures; sanitary requirements; furnishings and equipment; time schedules; play activities; routines of eating, sleeping, toileting, and washing; admission policies; and criteria for staff selection.

The well-being of a young child can only be assured if his or her total state of health is known, evaluated, and improved when necessary. Parents are, of course, the ones who have the long-range, continuing responsibility for their child's health and medical care. When, however, the day care center enters into a partnership with a parent for care of the child, the center shares responsibility not only for maintaining the child's health, but also for promoting it. The center has, in addition, an obligation to protect the health of the group as well as the individual. Unless proper controls are established, close daily contact of children carries with it the risk of spreading communicable disease.

To carry out its responsibility both to individuals and to the group, the day care center must have its own health program for the children. This should be in addition to, not instead of, whatever plans the parents may have. The center's health plan may either complement or augment that of the parents.

As with some other aspects of the day care program, the health plan that the center establishes may vary from one community to another, even from one center to another within the same community. It depends on the ages of the children being served, what community health and medical facilities—both public and private—are available, and how much parents use these facilities.

The ideal situation is one in which the family doctor (preferably a pediatrician) who has known the child for a long time shares knowledge of the child's development with the center's staff. The center's doctor, nurse, teachers, director, and social worker should know the child's physical condition in order to plan for special needs and to determine whether these needs can be met in a group setting.

If the child's family does not have its own doctor, it may be using the services of a community health center, a hospital outpatient department, or both. The center can collaborate with these institutions to obtain necessary developmental information about the child and to plan for ongoing health and medical care. When these services do not include medical care, the center can help the family obtain it as needed.

A few communities may have an extreme shortage of doctors or no public health facilities within reach. In such instances, the day care center may take direct responsibility for many health services that would otherwise be provided elsewhere.

When a center has been established to care for children with certain handicaps—physical or emotional—medical treatment may be a major part of the day-to-day program. This, of course, requires a specialized medical staff and specialized equipment.

The Health Team

To make sure that the health aspects of its program are medically sound, the center should have on its consultant staff a doctor and, if possible, a public health nurse. In the average day care center for well children, the doctor and the nurse usually serve on a part-time or consultant basis. A large center, or one whose program is planned for children with special needs, requires more of the medical staff's time. Usually, the center pays a fee for medical services, although occasionally a local public health agency makes the services available without cost.

The health team consists of the child's parents and the entire professional staff of the center—doctor, nurse, teachers, director, and social worker. Each has different responsibilities and different contributions to make toward promoting the child's health. Together they share a common concern for the child's total welfare, and together they have a common knowledge of all the child's experiences. It need hardly be emphasized that members of the health team must talk to each other, share information, and give professional advice as the situation indicates. A good health program involves joint planning by the team. This should be taken into account when making arrangements for consultation or part-time services of medical and nursing personnel; sufficient time must be allotted for them to meet with other staff members and with parents.

The Health Program

In most communities there are local regulations concerning the center's responsibility toward the children's health. Sometimes, however, these regulations are limited to public health aspects only. For the day care center to make certain that the children get the health and medical care they need and that they are protected as members of a group, its health plan should include the following policies and procedures:

Preadmission Physical Examination

Primarily, this examination is an appraisal of the child's health status. It should consist of a complete health history; current findings, including screenings for vision, hearing, and so forth; and an evaluative statement by the child's doctor. From it the center's physician and teachers can determine whether the day care center's program can benefit the child and whether attendance would jeopardize either the child or the group. The examination may be made by the child's own physician, by a community health facility, or by the center's staff physician. In any case, the examination record should become part of the center's files for future reference.

Immunization and Vaccinations

Certain immunizations should be required before a child can be admitted to a preschool or school group. These usually include protection against smallpox, diphtheria, whooping cough, poliomyelitis, measles, and tetanus. Others may be necessary in certain regions. A record of injections already given should be included with the preadmission examination report, and plans should be made for completing those still needed before admission. Plans should also be made for booster shots at required intervals. Whether these immunization and vaccination procedures are carried out in the day care center or by outside services again depends on the parent's health plan and the local situation.

Daily Health Inspection and Supervision

It is very important that a sick child not be admitted to the group, both for the child's sake and the group's, unless the day care center makes provision for the care of sick children. It is equally important that one member of the staff is aware at all times of each child's health status. The child's teacher is the best person to be responsible for both a daily morning inspection for obvious signs of illness and regular ongoing watchfulness over the child's general health. The teacher is the one who lives with the child during the hours at the center, knows how the child normally looks and behaves, and is quick to notice any changes. It is the teacher's job to note the changes and take appropriate action.

An emergency plan should be developed for each child. The plan should include the child's primary source of medical care, contact information for an individual who can be responsible for the child if the parents cannot be reached, written authorization from the parents for emergency medical treatment in the event the parents or other designated adults cannot be reached, and any other special instructions that may be necessary if the child becomes ill while in the care of the center. Unless the center has made provisions for the care of sick children, the teacher may ask the parent of a child who appears ill on arrival to take the child home. Before they leave, the teacher may check with the center's nurse or doctor, or, if neither is on the premises, suggest that the parent get medical care for the child. When a child shows signs of illness during the day, the teacher checks with the doctor or the nurse, if either is at the center; should the illness seem serious, the teacher immediately notifies the child's parents, and may also call the staff doctor or the child's family doctor.

Gradual changes in a child's appearance or behavior are brought to the attention of the parents and the center's physician, who takes whatever steps are necessary—talks to the parents, makes a medical referral, orders special tests, and so forth.

The teacher and other center staff members need training in order to recognize signs of illness and symptoms that may indicate health problems.

Private Space for the Sick Child

Children who become ill during the day must be removed from the group. This should be done so that the child feels as little sense of rejection as possible. The teacher cannot leave the group, but can arrange for another adult to be with or near the sick child. Parents should be called to pick up sick children as soon as possible, since children need their parents most when they are sick. Plans for such emergencies, which are bound to occur with the preschool child, should be worked out with the parents at the time the child enters the day care center.

Readmission after Sickness

When a child has been absent because of illness, it is desirable that the child be checked by a physician before returning to the group. Some centers require a doctor's certificate for readmission after every illness; others ask for it after a contagious illness. Often, as suggested by health authorities, children are readmitted only after they have been absent for the full period necessary for the particular disease to run its course. It is important to make clear to the parents that allowing a child to return to the center before he or she is really well hurts the child and may also present a risk to the group.

Control of Epidemics

If the children attending a day care center have been exposed to a communicable disease, parents must be told immediately. The staff physician and the local public health department should be notified and consultation requested regarding appropriate procedures to follow.

Accidents and First Aid

Every day care center's staff must be prepared to administer first aid for minor accidents and, in the case of a serious accident, know what to do and not to do while waiting for medical assistance. Staff training in first aid should be provided by the doctor, the nurse, or the local Red Cross. Staff members also should know whom to call when the center's physician or the child's family physician cannot be reached. The center must always know how to reach parents and should have the parents' written permission to obtain medical help in emergencies.

Periodic Physical Examinations

Every preschool child needs regular health checkups, including measurements of height and weight. Like the preadmission examination, these may be given by the staff physician, by the family physician, or by a public health facility. The information must be given to the staff, and a record must be kept at the center. Frequency of examination depends on the age and particular health condition of the child. Between ages three and five, two examinations a year are suggested, and one a year thereafter. More frequent examinations are necessary when a particular condition must be followed up.

Medical Care and Treatment

When medical care and follow-up treatment have been recommended as a result of a physical examination, the center should know whether the child is getting them. If necessary, the staff may help the parents obtain the care. The staff should also be informed by the parents, by the physician giving the treatment, or by both about any special precautions concerning the child's activities or diet. Medicines should not be administered at the center except by written order of the child's physician and with the written approval of the child's parents and the staff physician.

In the rare instance when a community has no facilities at all for medical care, the day care center should provide it. The center should also promote the setting up of medical facilities in the area.

Dental Examinations

Regular dental examinations are necessary for the preschool child, and the day care center staff should be prepared to help parents obtain regular examinations if they need assistance.

Mental Health Services

From time to time, the center may find it necessary to call on various mental health services to help a child who shows potentially serious problems of behavior or personality deviation. The center may have its own social work, psychiatric, and psychological staff on a part-time or consultant basis, or it may make referrals to community clinics and agencies. In either case, every staff member who has intimate knowledge of the child should work with the parents and the mental health professionals to help overcome the child's difficulties.

Food and Diet

Nutritious food is a most important contributing factor to the child's good health. Plans for food service must take into consideration how much time the child spends at the center and the child's general state of health and nutrition.

Food should be served at intervals sufficiently frequent to prevent excessive fatigue. (Young children are busy little people, expending energy almost all the time.) If the child is at the center most of the day, the center must supply a major part of the daily food requirements. Children cannot wait until they get home at the end of the day to have the hot meal they needed at noon. For the child who arrives very early and leaves very late, breakfast should be provided, and perhaps a light supper or snack at the end of the day, in addition to a hot meal at noon and other between-meal snacks.

To encourage eating, food should have a variety of textures and colors pleasing to children and be attractively served in a pleasant atmosphere. Whenever it is consistent with good nutrition, menu planning should consider local food tastes. Children like the familiar; even though we want them to acquire new tastes, it is a good idea for the menu to include, from time to time, a familiar and well-liked food. New foods can be introduced in dishes that have the seasonings or textures to which the children are accustomed.

Planning a balanced and suitable menu calls for the advice of a nutritionist as well as health personnel. Making the week's menus available to parents helps them plan their meals at home in relation to those of the center. Parents should also be asked about the eating habits of the family, as well as the individual food preferences of the child.

Hygiene and Sanitation

Everyone employed by the day care center should have preemployment and annual physical examinations, including chest X-rays and other tests indicated by local regulations or recommended by the staff physician. More frequent comprehensive examinations should be required for the kitchen staff. Under no circumstances should a sick cook be permitted in the kitchen. And it goes without saying that a sick teacher does not belong in the classroom any more than does a sick child.

Protective Aspects

When the day care center enters into a partnership with the parent and guarantees to provide supplementary care to enhance the child's growth, it also guarantees to take total responsibility for the child during the hours at the center. Although the teacher is not a substitute parent, while the child is in the center, the teacher performs certain functions of a parent and must be prepared to act in the parent's place when emergencies or unusual situations arise. Policies, regulations, and established procedures of the day care center should anticipate many of the problems a teacher may face and provide a framework within which the teacher has the freedom to act in emergencies.

This aspect of child care is called *custody*. The term is somewhat in disrepute in modern day care circles because it reminds people of the day nursery programs of many years ago, when custodial care was the only kind given. But custody really means "keeping." This is one of the things that the day care center does—keeps the child on its premises, safe from harm. Responsible "keeping" by a day care center has at least seven aspects.

Morning Admission

Even at an early hour in the morning, the parent should be able to turn over the child to a responsible individual whom the parent knows, inside the center's building, or, when transportation is provided, at the door of the car or bus. The child should never be left waiting alone in the street or playground. If this happens, the day care center should reassess its opening time to meet the needs of the parents it serves. The best procedure is for the parent to turn the child over to one of the child's own two teachers. When the center has a long day program and maintains a staggered schedule of arrival for teachers, a teacher from another group may greet the child at arrival. But it should always be a teacher—not the cook, a member of the maintenance staff, or a volunteer—who takes the child from the parents. If there are not enough teachers to cover the early hours, the center should not try to serve parents who must be at work very early, because it cannot serve them responsibly.

Departure

When it is time for the child to leave the center, the teacher—again, preferably the child's own—should release the child only to the parent or to someone authorized by the parent. If, in an emergency, the parent cannot come and sends an individual not known to the day care center staff, a note of permission in the parent's handwriting should be required. Very young brothers and sisters should not be permitted to take the child home unless this plan has been discussed with the parent and approved.

When the parent is late, the teacher should stay with the child until the parent arrives. If the parent does not come at all and cannot be reached, the center must take suitable action to provide overnight care for the child according to plans established for such emergencies.

In addition, the center should have a written policy, conforming to state and local regulations, stipulating actions to be taken if a parent who comes to pick up a child is unfit to do so because he or she is inebriated or under the influence of drugs. Usually this calls for summoning a relative or friend and providing extended care for the child until a safe conduct home is assured.

Unexpected Visitors

People who turn up at the center and claim to be visiting grandmothers, aunts, absent fathers, family friends, and so on should not be permitted to have any contact with the child unless by prearrangement with the parent who placed the child in the center. In any case, for the good of the child's routine, this kind of visiting should be discouraged, although the custodial parents should have open access to their children in the center at all times.

Accidents

As was pointed out earlier in this guide, the day care center must do everything possible to make certain that both building and activities are safe. If, in spite of all precautions, a child does have an accident, the center should be prepared to give the most responsible kind of care until the parent arrives, and, if necessary, to suggest how and where help can be obtained to continue the right care.

Emergencies

A formal plan should be established that outlines procedures to follow in the event of emergencies (personal and environmental), and includes community emergency telephone numbers. In the event of fire, flood, structural damage to the building, or other disaster that makes it necessary to evacuate the building, the staff should carry out the job as calmly and safely as possible, in the manner least frightening to children. The staff must stay with the children until their parents call for them. If, as in some types of disasters, the building is safe but the surrounding area is not, the staff must remain with the children in the building until their parents can get to them.

Keeping the Child during the Day

The teacher should always know how many of the children in the group are present and who they are. The experienced teacher counts noses automatically many times throughout the day, and especially whenever the group enters or leaves its classroom. An experienced teacher "feels" the children's presence and knows if a child has left the room. The teacher should not sit or stand facing away from the group for any length of time, and should be able to see most of the children all of the time, even though they may be playing in all four corners of the room.

A good day care center has two teachers for every group. When a child is missed or wanders out of the room alone, one of the teachers immediately goes to find the child.

As was pointed out in the section "A Safe Building," all dangerous exits from the building should be equipped with child-proof fasteners. Doors habitually left unlocked should have child-proof knobs—too high for a child to reach.

Aid and Comfort for the Child

During the course of the day, the teacher is aware not only of the child's health, but of everything that may affect the child's health and comfort. If the child's clothing is not warm enough for outdoor play, the teacher adds something from the center's supply. When the weather turns warm or the room becomes too hot, the teacher removes the child's sweater. The teacher fastens pants that are always falling down, ties a shoelace, helps the children protect their clothing during water play and handwashing, and changes clothes when they get wet. All this is done in a way that does not embarrass the child but protects the child's health and leaves him or her feeling comfortable.

Relationships between Parents and Day Care Center Staff

Up to the time the child comes to the day care center, parents are the most important people in his or her world. No matter how ready a child is to play with other children, it is a big step to leave the familiar confines of home. At the center the child enters a new environment and is confronted with strange adults, many other children, and the absence of the parents. This step can be made much easier if the child feels that the parents and the new teachers are friends. It can also be made much easier and more profitable if all of the adults involved—parents and staff members—are engaged in planning together those things that each of them can do to make the transition from home to center a smooth one.

But the need for joint planning does not stop with the child's admission to the center. Even if the child is at the center for as little as three hours a day, staff members must not forget that they are sharing care with the family. Everything that happens both at home and at the center has a tremendous influence on the child's life. It is well for the child if these two powerful influences are working together to give the child's life unity.

In the relationship between parents and staff members the child's old and new worlds meet. And it is here that the concept of day care as a supplement to the family's care of their children comes to life and takes on meaning. This relationship means that parents and staff will

- Share important information about the child and the child's experiences, past and present

- Arrive at mutually understood and agreed-upon goals for the child

- Be consistent in dealing with the child's behavior

- Take constructive action on problems growing out of the child's attendance at the day care center

- Recognize the day care center as a new, challenging environment where the child's previous life experiences can be made to serve the urge to grow

- Recognize the home as a place where the significance of the tremendous step forward made by the child entering the day care center must be understood, where adjustments are made to accommodate changing behavior, and where there will be sympathy for the inevitable growing pains

Practically speaking, how does this sharing of knowledge and planning take place at a day care center? Some of the ways are discussed in the following paragraphs.

Admission: The First Exchange of Information

Sharing information begins when the parents first come to the day care center to apply for admission. Parents may already have a well-formed impression of what the center can do for their child and for them as parents. Even if they do not, they almost surely have an objective in mind. Here begins the exchange of information about the child, the family, the parents' objectives, and the program and policies of the day care center. This process results in a joint decision by parents and center staff on whether the child is to be admitted.

Before the decision is made, several staff members will have to be involved. A doctor's evaluation of the child's health will be one decisive factor. The teacher's evaluation of the child's readiness and ability to fit into the group will also be decisive, particularly when the child has a handicap or a health history that indicates caution.

This decision is not made during the first meeting between parents and staff unless it is a negative one for easily established reasons, such as the age of the child (too old or too young), hours of care that do not fit the parents' needs, or their inability to pay fees, if required. Whenever a child is refused for any reason, the center's staff should be capable of making referrals to other community resources that fit the family situation and the child's needs. The staff member who interviews parent applicants should have the skill to evaluate a situation and a knowledge of community resources to make appropriate referrals.

If the child is accepted, the staff can be of great help to the parents by giving advance warning about some of the problems that may develop simply because the child has entered the center. The parents, usually without previous experience with a day care center, do not know what to expect. The center's staff members, however, have worked with hundreds of children and can predict fairly well what will happen. Not only does preparing the parents for the child's reactions help them to handle the transition better, but it also comforts parents to know that their child is not the only one who has an adjustment to make.

Sometimes a parent plans to start working at the same time that his or her child enters the center. The child will almost surely have a reaction to two such big changes happening simultaneously. If, at the time of application, the staff discusses with the parent the probable effect of these changes, the parent may be able to defer going to work until the child has a chance to settle down in the day care center.

The arrival of a new baby is also not the most propitious moment for a child to leave home for the first time, even for a few hours a day. Many young parents need help to understand this and to plan for the day care center experience to begin either before or after the new baby is born.

Parents should be encouraged to spend as much time at the center as their child needs during the first days there in order to build a bridge between home and "school." When necessary, offer help with practical arrangements to make this possible. The parents are the child's link to home, and their presence helps the child adjust more easily. Taking the child home early for the first few days also helps. This arrangement can usually be worked out, if it is planned, even with working parents. Many employers are sympathetic to the needs of children and will cooperate.

During the child's first days at the center, the teachers and other staff members must be especially sensitive to the child's reaction to this new world. Even a child who is old enough and mature enough to enjoy playing with other children may show regressive behavior at first. The change in behavior may take place at home or in the center, depending on the child. Both parents and teachers should understand this and be prepared to handle it. When the teacher knows how the child is reacting at home, he or she may be able to arrange the child's program at the center to meet any special needs.

Some young children, for example, find group participation very exciting, and may be overtired by the stimulation. The teacher can plan for these children to have extra rest during the day and some periods of quiet activity somewhat apart from the group until they become accustomed to having other children around. The parents can be helped to arrange for their child to have more rest at home and to be patient if the child is irritable from excessive fatigue. If the child seems upset by the separation from the parents, the parent and the teacher can discuss ways for each to give the child more individual attention. They may also plan together to shorten the day in the center for a while. Sometimes the child develops fears of being deserted by the parents soon after admission to the center. The teacher, the parents, and the social worker can help the child overcome these fears. If the child continues to suffer from separation from the parents, the center director can be helpful to the parents and child. In some instances the director may help the parents make other, more suitable arrangements.

Continuing Relationships between Parents and Staff

The need for two-way communication between parents and staff members does not stop when the child has finally settled down. The child is growing and changing all the time, so the child's behavior and needs are changing as well. The staff must be alert to these changes and to the reactions of the parents, since many parents, in spite of what they say, find it difficult to share their child with another adult. Events at home also affect the child—a new baby, moving to another house, a sick father or mother, a parent's loss of a job, difficulties with an older brother or sister. The center's staff needs to know about these problems in order to help the child. The staff should give the parents the feeling that they can come in to discuss such problems, that there is a warm interest in them as persons, and that skilled help is available if needed.

All parents should be able to look to the day care center for assistance with problems and practices in childrearing. The team of teachers, social workers, doctors, and nurses on the center's staff should be expert in childrearing and should use their contacts with parents to influence practices in the home.

Group Activities among Parents

Parents should be able to exchange ideas with other parents at the day care center. Exchanges help them to develop a more objective view of their own child and to realize how much their child has in common with other children of the same age. Group meetings of parents, with discussions on topics of interest to them, are another means of strengthening the relationship between the center and the parents. Parents should, of course, be consulted about the subjects they want to discuss and the most suitable times for the discussions. Sometimes parents enjoy purely social occasions. They also enjoy raising money through their own efforts for a project that will enrich the lives of the children in the center. Sometimes they like to contribute talents, services, or materials to the center directly.

Individual Contacts

Group activities can never take the place of individual talks between the parents and various staff members. Talks are necessary for planning and sharing information about the child; they may be casual, as in the day-to-day contacts when the child is brought to the center and taken home, or they may be arranged in advance, so that a talk will be uninterrupted.

Home visiting can be another way of sharing information and bringing the child's two worlds together. Children love to have their teachers and social workers visit their homes. Most parents like it, too, if the visit is a friendly one with no connotations of prying or authoritarian attitudes. When a child is sick, a visit may be especially welcomed by the family, and the teacher or the social worker making the visit may gain new and important insights about the child in the home setting.

The importance of this continuing relationship between parents and staff is that it makes both aware that they are partners in the care and education of the child, and that the job is not easy on either side. Staff members should feel neither defensive nor superior. They as well as the parents face moments of uncertainty about the real needs of the child and about what steps to take to help the child. Conferences between parents and staff members become meaningful when both recognize their need for the other and consciously combine efforts to overcome difficulties and make the child's life wholesome and happy.

Reaching Out to Parents

Day-to-day contact with the parents who bring their children to the center and pick them up is the easiest way to keep the relationship between parents and staff members strong and vital. Daily contact also makes the child feel that the people in his or her two worlds are friends. When the center provides transportation, however, daily contact is not possible; therefore, staff members and parents must plan for conferences and for parents' visits to the center. Children enjoy having parents visit the classroom, and the visits provide a good opportunity for the parents to see what the children are doing and learning and to compare their child to other children of the same age. Classroom visits are good for all parents in any day care center, but they are especially necessary when parents do not have daily contact with the center.

Some day care centers serve many parents too overburdened with work schedules and the care of children to visit the center often or even to accompany their child to the center. In such instances, the center may be able to initiate cooperative arrangements. If a parent has exacting job requirements or other children who cannot be left alone, center parents or volunteers may offer to take the day care child to the center and to keep younger children on conference days.

It often takes special efforts and new, imaginative ways of reaching out to parents to enable parents and children to fully enjoy the benefits of day care.

Appendix A: Suggested Furnishings, Equipment, and Supplies

The following list is intended only as a guide to the variety of items, their dimensions, and the quantities that may be needed in a day care center for young children. It is neither all-inclusive nor minimal. The construction of the premises, the number of children, and the size of the staff have a bearing on which items are needed and on the quantities of each.

The center's budget will also influence its selections from this list. Where the budget is limited, the emphasis should be put on three basic kinds of equipment:

1. Comfortable, durable furniture

2. Educational materials that help a child to be creative and imaginative

3. Equipment and materials that stimulate cooperative play and social experiences

It is important to note that this list does not give recognition to the differing abilities and interests of children at different age levels. Although all of the suggested items are suitable for ages three to five years, some of them are suitable for only one age level, and others will be needed in different quantities depending on the ages of the children in the group. This is a matter for the professionally qualified teacher to determine.

Basic Furnishings and Equipment

Furnishings for Each Classroom

Window shades to dim light at naptime

Window screens

Guards for windows on the second floor and above

Guards for radiators or other heating equipment

Tables to seat four or six children, 1½ square feet minimum per child, with washable tops

- 18" high for 3-year-olds

- 20" and 22" high for 4- and 5-year-olds

Chairs, one for each child

- 10" from seat to floor for 3-year-olds

- 12" and 14" from seat to floor for 4- and 5-year-olds

Storage space for each playroom—open shelves in sections, movable and with backs, for play materials, not over 26" high, 12" deep, 12" between shelves (Allow approximately 1' per child.)

Coat lockers, one for each child, with hooks or pegs for hanging coats, hats, etc., 12" wide, 12" deep

- 9" of vertical space for hats

- 32" to 36" minimum vertical space for coats

- 9" vertical space for shoes and boots

Closet space for supplies (including wide shelves for easel paper, etc.) and for blankets and cots

Space for teaching materials and extra emergency clothing for children, space for teachers' outdoor clothing

Bulletin boards or suitable wall space, at child level, for hanging pictures and children's paintings

Bulletin boards or suitable wall space, at adult level (may be in hall or office)

Screens, 36" x 48" (on 14" base), to separate quiet and active play areas; to separate cots at rest time (Low, movable shelves may be substituted.)

Wastebaskets, durably constructed

Pictures, plants, and other items to create a homelike atmosphere

Individual rugs or mats, washable, for resting

Chairs for visitors

Fire extinguishers and smoke detectors, as required by local regulations

Extra clothing for emergencies, especially such items as mittens, boots, sweaters, caps, socks, shirts, pants, and underwear, in addition to regular items supplied by parents

Room thermometer

Clock

Facial tissues

For Sleeping

Cots that can be stacked, one for each child, 12" from floor, 27" x 54" for 3-, 4-, and 5-year-olds, 27" x 62" for large 5-year-olds (All cots and bedding should be marked and stored for individual use.)

Blankets, warm for cold weather, cotton or flannelette for mild weather, 36" x 60"

Cotton sheets, contour preferable; top sheet optional, 36" x 60"

Waterproof sheeting, same size as cots, for children who need it

For Washroom and Toilet

Washbowls, approximately 24" from floor or platform, minimum of 1 for 15 children and 2 to a group, fastened securely

Mirrors over washbasins

Flush toilets, 12" to 14" from floor or platform, minimum of 1 for 10 children and 2 to a group

Toilet seat insets, adjustable, for children who need them

Toilet paper container and toilet paper within children's reach from each toilet

Soap for washbasins

Paper towel container and towels

Diaper changing surface, with disposable moisture-proof covers to be changed after every use

Diapers

Disposable wipes for cleansing diaper area

Closed container for disposal of covers, wipes, and disposable diapers

High cabinet or shelf for teachers' use

Bath towels for emergencies or for summer showers

Mop and pail for spilled water or for toilet accidents

For Drying Clothing

Clothes racks or lines located in warm place, or automatic dryer

For Food Service

Food-carrier cart, with shelves, 1 for each group

Place mats (optional if tables are sanitary and attractively finished)

Plates, luncheon size

Shallow bowls for soup

Dessert saucers

Tumblers or cups, for snacks as well as for lunch

Teaspoons

Forks, small size, with blunt prongs

Knives for adults

Pitchers

Casseroles, covered

Serving spoons

Paper napkins

For Meal Preparation (Kitchen Equipment)

Stove with oven and at least 4 burners

Microwave oven

Double sink with 2 drainboards (check with local health department on requirements for dishwashing, sterilization, food storage, and so forth); dishwasher desirable

Sink for washing hands

Refrigerator, capacity of 45 to 60 cubic feet recommended

Closets, cupboards, or adjoining pantry with drawers and shelves large enough for quantity storage

Kettles with covers, 6 to 10 quart capacity

Saucepans, 1 to 6 quart

Baking pans, 15¼" x 10½" x 2½"

Double boilers, 3 and 4 quart

Skillet, iron, 10½" x 2"

Teakettle, 4 quart

Coffee maker

Strainer, coarse, 8" diameter

Colander

Egg beater, rotary

Food processor

Mixing bowls, 1 to 6 quart

Flour sifter

Containers or bins with tightly fitting covers for salt, sugar, and flour

Measuring cups, 1 cup and 1 pint sizes

Large bread container

Grater

Can opener

Chopping board

Potato masher

Kitchen knives, three sizes

Spatula

Kitchen forks with heat-resistant handles

Spoons, measuring, mixing, and 14" wooden

Clock

Sink strainer

Dishpan, 12 quart enamel

Dish drainer, wire, 16¾" x 12¼"

Vegetable brushes

Pitchers, 2 quart

Scales, kitchen

Trays, 17¾" x 13⅞"

Wastecan for garbage, 5 gallon, with cover; garbage disposal unit desirable

Wastebasket

Soaps, cleansers, etc.

Dish towels

Dishcloths and cloths for cleaning

Pot holders

Electric potato peeler, mixer, and large-size toaster desirable

For First-Aid Room

Working telephone with emergency numbers and note pad and pen

Table and chairs, adult size and child size

Supply cabinet with lock

Cot with bedding, one or more

Soft washable toys and other comfort items

Lamp and/or flashlight

Wastebasket with cover

Disposable nonporous gloves

Scissors

Tweezers

Thermometer

Bandage tape

Sterile gauze pads

Flexible roller gauze

Triangular bandage

Safety pins

Cold pack

Tongue depressors

First aid supplies as recommended by consulting physician

First aid text such as Red Cross, American Academy of Pediatrics, or equivalent

Toilet, covered laundry receptacle, and washing supplies—should be accessible

For Housekeeping and Cleaning

Mops

Pails

Fiber brooms

Push brooms

Dust pans, long handle

Cloths for general cleaning and dusting

Scrub brushes

Soap, soap powder, floor and wall cleaners, cleanser, and so on

Vacuum cleaner (desirable)

For Staff Lounge or Library

Desk or table

Straight chairs, 1 or more

Easy chairs

Couch

Bookcase or shelves for reference books, professional magazines

Lamps

Bulletin board

Wastebasket

Rug (optional)

For Offices and Meeting Rooms

Sufficient space for director and supervisory and clerical staff, and to provide privacy for interviews and for staff, board, and committee meetings

Telephone

Desks

Conference table and chairs

Lamps

Bookcases or shelves

Locked file cabinets

Computer and printer and/or typewriter

Copying machine

Calculator

Fax machine (desirable)

Office Supplies

Identification tags and stickers

Tape dispensers and tape

Scissors

Stapler

Paper clips

Needles and thread

Safety pins

Rubber bands

Pencils and pens

Ruler, yardstick, and measuring tape

Stationery, bond paper, notebooks and note pads, and so on

Copier paper

Thumbtacks

Glue and rubber cement

Record folders and materials

- Application forms

- Health record forms

- Individual progress reports

Play Equipment and Materials

Outdoor Play Equipment

Climbing structures

- Free-form tunnel or cave

- 3-way ladder or a jungle gym
- Double horizontal bar for 5-year-olds, approximately 35" to 45" high

Trapeze bar on rope chain, adjustable height and length

Swing apparatus

- Swings, detachable, with canvas, leather, or rubber seats

Balance beam, low

Slide no higher than 6' 6" with protective sides at the top

Packing boxes

- 48" x 30" x 30"
- 35" x 23" x 16"

Rocking boat

Collapsible play tunnel

Hollow blocks

- 5½" x 5½" x 11"
- 5½" x 11" x 11"
- 5½" x 11" x 22"

Building boards, 5½" x ½" x 36"

Three-wheel riding toys with soft edges, low wheel base

Wagons, good size for loading and riding

Wheelbarrow, medium size

Toy trucks and cars, all sizes

Balls

Jump ropes

Sleds, small size (flying saucers recommended)

Snow shovels

Brooms, child size

Digging area and/or sandbox, deep, approximately 10' x 10' or larger

Sand toys: spoons, shovels, scoops, pails, strainers, kitchen pans, and so on

Brushes for water painting

Pails, non-rusting

Watering cans

Step ramp

Tub for water play

Source of water for sand and water play

Shower or spray for use in warm weather

Wading pool with drain

Variety of salvage material, such as tire tubes, short lengths of garden hose, cable spools—desirable

Indoor Play Equipment
(Some of this may be used outdoors in warm weather.)

Blocks, hollow

- 5½" x 5½" x 11"
- 5½" x 11" x 11"
- 5½" x 11" x 22"

Unit blocks

- Units, 1⅜" x 2¾" x 5½"

- Half units

- Double units

- Quadruple units

- Pillars

- Small cylinders

- Large cylinders

- Large triangles

- Curves

- X-switches

- Y-switches

- Roof boards

Wooden animals and people, wide base, scaled to proportionate sizes

Wooden or plastic table construction sets

For Water Play

Water table

Funnels, measuring cups, containers

Several small boats and other floating toys

Water wheel

Water pump

Aprons

Sponge and mop

Manipulation Toys

Wooden puzzle inlays, 5 to 20 pieces

Puzzle box

Picture lotto games

Flannel board sets

Pounding beds, wooden mallets

Nest of blocks, 6", 7", 8", 10"

Color cone

Peg board with pegs 1" or longer

Peg boards with variety of shapes and sizes

Hammer-and-nail beds

Cash register

Beads, wooden, 1"

Shoestrings for stringing beads

Interlocking blocks or logs and other construction toys

Transportation Toys

Trains, interlocking, wooden (flat bottom)

Train, interlocking, wooden, with wheels, no removable pieces

Train, large with wheels

Cars, trucks, airplanes, boats, medium size

Submarines

Spaceships

For Doll Play and Housekeeping

Doll bed, large enough to hold a child, bedding

Doll carriage, not collapsible, large enough to hold a child

Doll bureau or dresser, 24" to 30" high

Doll high chair

Rocking chair, child size

Small table

Chairs

Unbreakable tea party dishes, 6 pieces and tray

Toy stove, child size (not doll size), approximately 24" high, 23" long, 12" wide

Sink, child size, approximately 24" high, with pan for water

Toy refrigerator, child size, approximately 26" high

Cooking utensils, child size

Kitchen cabinet, shelf, or other storage unit

Broom, child size

Dustpan

Mop, child size

Ironing board

Irons (not electric)

Clothespins and clothesline

Baskets

Toy telephones

Dolls, cuddly, boy and girl

Dolls, washable and nonbreakable, boy and girl, 10" to 20"

Doll clothes, loose fitting, large, with large buttonholes or fasteners

Several animals, soft, cuddly, washable

Dress-up clothes (men's and women's): hats, shoes, pocketbooks, etc.

Box, chest, or clothes rack for dress-up clothes

Art Supplies

Easel, double, with wide trough to hold paint jars

Paint jars, plastic (Small yogurt containers are ideal.)

Brushes, long-handled

- Bristles ½" wide

- Bristles 1" wide

Jar and cover for clay

Scissors, good quality

- Blunt

- Pointed

Aprons, heavy toweling or waterproof material

Newsprint, 24" x 30"

Construction paper, 12" x 18"

Colored paper, 9" x 12" or 12" x 18"

- Orange

- Black

- Red

- Green

- Blue, medium

- Yellow

Finger paint paper, 18" x 24"

Finger paints[9]

- Red

- Yellow

- Blue

- Green

Easel paint (powder)

- Red

- Yellow

- Blue

- Green

- Black

- Brown

Paste, washable and nontoxic

Clay, moist preferred

Playdough (to supplement clay, not to replace it)

Rolling pins, cookie cutters, molds

Crayons, large, ⅜" diameter

Stencils

Rulers

Wrapping paper, brown, approximately 20" wide

---

[9] Finger paint recipes: (1) Bring 5 cups of water to a boil. Dissolve 2 cups of cornstarch with small amount of cold water, add to boiling water, and stir in 12 teaspoons glycerine (optional). Add 2 cups of white soap flakes, stir until smooth, and let the mixture cool. Add poster paint for color. Makes 3½ quarts of finger paint. (2) Add poster paint or powdered tempera to liquid laundry starch until desired color is obtained. Stir and store.

Oilcloth (for finger paint, and for table and floor protection when necessary)

Pieces of linoleum

Carpentry Supplies

Sturdy, well-made workbench with vise and clamps

Hammers, 13 or 16 ounce, good balance, flat heads

Crosscut saw, 12"

Screwdrivers

Pliers

Rack for hanging up tools (out of children's casual reach)

Plastic safety goggles

Nails, large headed, roofing

Nails, assorted sizes

Sandpaper, 9" x 10½", #0 to #1½

Mill ends of soft wood and semifinished lumber, up to 3' lengths

Assortment of button molds and beads for wheels

Science

Aquarium with plants, seaweed, fish, and food

Large pet cage with galvanized removable tray, to house small pets for short periods

Pots, bowls, and trays for flowers, growing plants

Watering cans

Potting materials and tools

Additional materials such as the following: leaves, acorns, stones, bulbs, seeds, with box planters and wide-mouth jars for planting

For 4- and 5-year-olds: magnets, prism, magnifying glass, etc.

Music

Drums (without sticks)

Bells, jingle (wrist)

Rhythm sticks

Triangle, for 4- and 5-year-olds

Tambourines, for 4- and 5-year-olds

Cymbals, for 5-year-olds

Piano

Record player or tape deck

Records or tapes

Story and Picture Books

A carefully selected, multicultural collection for young children, meeting the requirements of the various age levels and including the following categories: transportation, birds and animals, science, holiday seasons, nonsense rhymes and stories, Mother Goose rhymes, folktales from various cultures, and family life.

In addition, the center should have several anthologies of poems and stories to tell. Advice and books on loan may be obtained from the children's division of the local public library.

Appendix B: Suggested Readings

Adams, Gina C. *Who Knows How Safe? The Status of State Efforts to Ensure Quality Child Care.* Washington, DC: Children's Defense Fund, 1990.

Albrecht, Kay M., and Plantz, Margaret C., ed. *Developmentally Appropriate Practice in School-Age Child Care Programs.* Alexandria, VA: American Home Economics Association, 1991.

Aronson, Susan S. *Health and Safety in Child Care.* New York: Harper Collins, 1991.

Bredekamp, Sue, ed. *Accreditation Criteria and Procedures of the National Academy of Early Childhood Programs.* Washington, DC: National Association for the Education of Young Children, 1991.

Bredekamp, Sue, ed. *Developmentally Appropriate Practice in Early Childhood Programs Serving Children from Birth through Age 8.* Washington, DC: National Association for the Education of Young Children, 1987.

Chehrazi, Shahla S., M.D., ed. *Psychosocial Issues in Day Care.* Washington, DC: American Psychiatric Press, Inc., 1990.

Child Care Information Exchange, The Directors' Magazine. Redmond, WA: Exchange Press, Inc. Bimonthly.

Child Welfare League of America Standards for Excellence for Child Day Care Services. Washington, DC: Child Welfare League of America, 1992.

CWLA Salary Study. Washington, DC: Child Welfare League of America, 1991.

Facility Design for Early Childhood Programs Resource Guide. Washington, DC: National Association for the Education of Young Children, 1991.

Guidelines on Productive Employment of Older Adults in Child Care Programs. Pittsburgh, PA: Generations Together, 1991.

Helping Children Love Themselves and Others: A Resource Guide to Equity Materials for Young Children. Washington, DC: The Children's Foundation, 1991.

Howes, Carollee. *Keeping Current in Child Care Research: An Annotated Bibliography.* Washington, DC: National Association for the Education of Young Children, 1990.

Kisker, Ellen Eliason; Hofferth, Sandra L.; Phillips, Deborah A.; and Farquhar, Elizabeth. *A Profile of Child Care Settings: Early Education and Care in 1990.* Washington, DC: U.S. Department of Education, 1991.

Miller, Darla. *First Steps toward Cultural Differences: Socialization in Infant/Toddler Day Care.* Washington, DC: Child Welfare League of America, 1989.

Preparing a Personnel Policy Manual. Washington, DC: Child Welfare League of America, 1991.

Preparing Practitioners to Work with Infants, Toddlers, and their Families. Washington, DC: National Center for Clinical Infant Programs, 1990.

"School-Age Child Care Technical Assistance Papers." Albany, NY: New York State Council on Children and Families. Issued periodically.

Serving Children with HIV Infection in Child Day Care: A Guide for Center-Based and Family Day Care Providers. Washington, DC: Child Welfare League of America, 1991.

Status of Day Care in Canada. Ottawa: Health and Welfare Canada, 1990.

Whitebrook, Marcy; Phillips, Deborah; and Howes, Carollee. *Who Cares? Child Care Teachers and the Quality of Care in America: Final Report of the National Child Care Staffing Study.* Oakland, CA: Child Care Employees Project, 1990.

Willer, Barbara; Hofferth, Sandra L.; Kisker, Ellen Eliason; Divine-Hawkins, Patricia; Farquhar, Elizabeth; and Glantz, Frederic B. *The Demand and Supply of Child Care in 1990.* Washington, DC: National Association for the Education of Young Children, 1991.

Young Children, Journal of the National Association for the Education of Young Children. Washington, DC: National Association for the Education of Young Children. Monthly.

Appendix C: Organizations Publishing Resource Materials on Child Day Care Centers and Programs for Young Children

American Academy of Pediatrics
141 Northwest Boulevard
Elk Grove Village, IL 60007

American Public Health Association
1015 15th Street NW
Washington, DC 20005

Bank Street College of Education
 Center for Children's Policy
610 West 112th Street
New York, NY 10025

Canadian Child Day Care Federation
120 Holland Avenue, Suite 401
 Ottawa, Ontario K1Y OX6

Child Care Action Campaign
330 Seventh Avenue, 18th Floor
New York, NY 10001

Child Care Employee Project
6536 Telegraph Avenue, A-201
Oakland, CA 94609

Child Care Information Exchange
P.O. Box 2890
Redmond, WA 98073

Child Care Law Center
22 Second Street, 5th Floor
San Francisco, CA 94105.

Child Welfare League of America
440 First Street NW, Suite 310
Washington, DC 20001-2085

Children's Defense Fund
122 C Street NW
Washington, DC 20001

*Clearinghouse on Implementation
of Child Care and Eldercare
Services*
Women's Bureau
U.S. Department of Labor,
Washington, DC 20210

*Council for Early Childhood
Professional Recognition*
1718 Connecticut Avenue NW
Washington, DC 20009

Ecumenical Child Care Network
475 Riverside Drive, Room 572
New York, NY 10115

*ERIC Clearinghouse on Early
Childhood Education*
University of Illinois
805 West Pennsylvania Avenue
Urbana, IL 61810

*Frank Porter Graham Child Devel-
opment Center*
CB #8180
University of North Carolina at
Chapel Hill
Chapel Hill, NC 27599.

*High/Scope Educational Research
Foundation*
600 North River Street
Ypsilanti, MI 48198

Merrill-Palmer Institute
71-A East Ferry
Wayne State University
Detroit, MI 48202

*National Association for the Educa-
tion of Young Children*
8134 Connecticut Avenue NW
Washington, DC 20009

*National Association of Child Care
Resource and Referral Agencies*
2116 Campus Drive SE
Rochester, MN 55904.

*National Association of State
Boards of Education*
1012 Cameron Street
Alexandria, VA 22314.

*National Black Child Development
Institute*
1463 Rhode Island Avenue NW
Washington, DC 20005

*National Center for Clinical Infant
Programs*
2000 14th Street North, Suite 380
Arlington, VA 22201-2500

*National Jewish Early Childhood
Network*
Bureau of Jewish Education
6505 Wiltshire Boulevard
Los Angeles, CA 90048.

Pacific Oaks College
714 West California Boulevard
Pasadena, CA 91105

*Resources for Child Care Manage-
ment*
261 Springfield Avenue
Berkeley Heights, NJ 07922

School Age Child Care Project
Wellesley College Center for
    Research on Women
Wellesley, MA 02181

Wheelock College
200 The Riverway
Boston, MA 02215

*Yale Bush Center in Child Develop-
    ment and Social Policy*
P.O. Box 11A Yale Station
New Haven, CT 06520